THE CLUB, THE BALL . . .
THE OBSESSION!

This hilarious volume, filled with outrageous illustrations, will not improve your stance, teach you how to find your ball in a sand trap, or even uncover the deep mystery to getting a hole-in-one every time. But it will make you laugh out loud as you venture into the world of the golfer. You'll learn about:

How to really "tee" off a golfer

•

20 things to do with an old golf club

•

Sex and the single golfer

•

10 reasons golf is so popular

•

The mental side of golf

•

And much, much more

RICHARD MINTZER is the author of two other books in the Plume Unofficial Handbook series. He is a humor and comedy writer who teaches humor-writing seminars in Manhattan. His articles have appeared in *US, Playbill,* and *American Baby.* He lives in New York City. Don't ask about his handicap.

THE UNOFFICIAL
GOLFER'S
HANDBOOK

Richard Mintzer

A PLUME BOOK

PLUME
Published by the Penguin Group
Penguin Books USA Inc., 375 Hudson Street,
New York, New York 10014, U.S.A.
Penguin Books Ltd, 27 Wrights Lane,
London W8 5TZ, England
Penguin Books Australia Ltd, Ringwood,
Victoria, Australia
Penguin Books Canada Ltd, 2801 John Street,
Markham, Ontario, Canada L3R 1B4
Penguin Books (N.Z.) Ltd, 182–190 Wairau Road,
Auckland 10, New Zealand

Penguin Books Ltd, Registered Offices:
Harmondsworth, Middlesex, England

First published by Plume,
an imprint of New American Library,
a division of Penguin Books USA Inc.

First Printing, August, 1991
10 9 8 7 6 5 4 3 2 1

 REGISTERED TRADEMARK—MARCA REGISTRADA

LIBRARY OF CONGRESS CATALOGING IN PUBLICATION DATA
Mintzer, Richard.
    The unofficial golfer's handbook / by Richard Mintzer.
      p.   cm.

  ISBN 0-452-26641-6
    1. Golf—Humor.   2. Golf—Anecdotes.   I. Title.
  GV967.M56   1991
  796.352'0207—dc20   90-27904
                                                   CIP

Printed in the United States of America
Set in Memphis Medium and Video

BOOKS ARE AVAILABLE AT QUANTITY DISCOUNTS WHEN USED TO PROMOTE PRODUCTS OR
SERVICES. FOR INFORMATION PLEASE WRITE TO PREMIUM MARKETING DIVISION, PENGUIN
BOOKS USA INC., 375 HUDSON STREET, NEW YORK, NEW YORK, 10014.

Contents
or
What's On the Course?

4th Hole—

On the Course......45

5th Hole—

Nobody Said It Was Easy.....67

6th Hole—

Places to Swing........75

7th Hole—

"Real" Golfers......93

8th Hole—

Off the
Course 101

9th Hole—

Potpourri 111

1st HOLE—

What Is Golf?

A game in which one endeavors to control a ball with implements ill adapted for such purposes.

—Woodrow Wilson

Are You Obsessed with Golf?
—A Quiz

1. Do you bring a putter and a couple of balls when visiting a cemetery?

2. Do you find yourself contemplating your neighbor's front lawn to determine how fast or slow it is?

3. Does every pair of pants that you own, including the ones that go with your tuxedo, have golf tees in the pockets?

4. Do you hold your fork with an overlapping grip?

5. Do all of your shoes, sneakers, and bedroom slippers have cleats on the bottom?

6. Do you yell "FORE!" during sex just prior to orgasm?

7. Is every pencil in your home (and office) less than 6 inches long?

8. Do your winter gloves have Velcro fasteners?

9. Do you refer to 8 inches of rain in your basement as casual water?

10. At the bank, do you let the person farthest away from the teller go first?

If your answers to any of the preceding questions were yes, you are indeed obsessed with golf.

Glossary

GOLFER'S DICTIONARY

ACE—See "Hole In One!" More frequently used in bar talk than seen in reality.

ADDRESS—In the words of Art Carney as Ed Norton, to address the ball is to say "Hello, Ball." Actually it's the position you assume to strike the ball before golf lessons teach you a better position.

ALBATROSS—Your partner whose great score is ruining your day. Also a double eagle or playing with your spouse.

AWAY—This refers to the ball lying farthest from the hole. It also refers to where your caddie can go after handing you the wrong club.

BACKSPIN—Something the average golfer has only heard about.

BANANA BALL—A ball that either travels in a long left to right arc, is yellow, or is eaten by a chimpanzee.

BIRDIE—That which flies overhead without a disruptive engine noise, or a hole made in one under par. One reason for living.

BLIND HOLE—A hole where the green is hidden from view. Also, a hole where you'd probably have better luck if you hit blindfolded.

BOGEY—Par for most mere mortals. The star of *Casablanca*.

BREAK—The slant or slope of the green that makes the ball go everywhere but where you want it to.

BUNKER—A sand trap or small hill intended to cause premature gray hair or balding.

CADDIE—Someone to blame your mistakes on.

CARPET—The green, or that little piece of "hair" flapping in the wind every time your partner goes into his backswing.

CLEEK—The number 4 wood, and the sound your golf shoes make if worn in your kitchen or in the clubhouse.

DIVOT—A chunk of the ground torn from the course, on your shot, which inevitably travels farther than your ball. The first dozen or so should be replaced. Beyond that, the golfer should be replaced.

DOGLEG—A hole that often takes a great deal of time to play, because it's designed to curve in one direction so that you will usually attempt an "over the trees" shortcut and spend 15 minutes ball hunting.

DOUBLE BOGEY—The most familiar term among weekend golfers.

DRIVE—Your reason for renting an electric cart. Also the shot to start a hole, also known as a tee shot or the beginning of your nightmare.

DRIVER—The number 1 wood or the guy behind the wheel of the cart.

DUFFER—Someone who brags about a triple bogey for the rest of the week. Also your spouse's uncle who swore he'd played once back in 1962.

EAGLE—A patriotic symbol. Also two under par—see Fantasy.

EXPLOSION SHOT—A shot hit by a terrorist. Also a shot out of a sand trap that gets sand on everyone.

FAIRWAY—The well-manicured portion of the course, rarely used by most golfers.

FANTASY—A hole in one; an eagle; playing par at Pebble Beach.

FLAG—Gives you a destination so you don't simply hit the ball around forever.

FLASH TRAP—A small shallow bunker for quickly exposing yourself to golfers of the opposite sex.

FORE—Roughly means "Look out!" "Heads up!" and "Oh shit" all in one word.

FOURSOME—Four people teamed willingly (or more often unwillingly) to play golf together.

GIMME—A shot that is so easy you don't even have to take it and humiliate yourself by missing it.

GROSS SCORE—The score you don't admit to having just gotten on the round.

HACKER—Someone whose divots far outnumber their yardage on a consistent basis.

HANDICAP—An allowance of strokes designed so you can play with people far superior to you. Also, a system whereby the 18 holes are rated in order of difficulty by someone having a somewhat different perspective of the course than yourself.

HAZARD—A hacker with a club in his or her hands. Also, someone driving a golf cart or anything that gets in your way on or near the course while playing a hole.

HOLE IN ONE!—A miracle that you have the legal right to talk about on a daily basis for the rest of your life.

HONOR—The privilege of giving the rest of your foursome a good look at "what not to do" on the hole as you "lead off."

HOOK—Fishing gear. Also a ball that, of its own volition, chooses to make a sharp left turn while in flight and leave its designated route.

LATERAL HAZARD—A water hazard alongside of you that never seems to go away.

LIE—What golfers use to improve their scores. Also, the position where your ball sits on the ground before you nudge it slightly onto the top of the grass.

LINE—The direction in which the player wishes the ball would have gone just after hitting it. What you might find at the clubhouse bathrooms. Something you tell the golf pro so he thinks you play well.

LINK—A synonym for a golf course and the name of a character on the old "Mod Squad" TV series.

LOFT—A large, open living space with plenty of room to practice indoors. Also, the angle of the clubhouse or to hit a shot with a high trajectory.

MATCH PLAY—Competition designed so that you lose money on each hole rather than simply on the entire course.

MULLIGAN—That second shot that nobody saw you take.

NET SCORE—When a professional basketball player in New Jersey plays golf. Also, your score minus your handicap and cheating.

OUT OF BOUNDS—Landing your shot in a nearby Fotomat.

OVERCLUBBING—Accidentally hitting the ball to Cambodia.

PAR—Someone's sadistic idea of how many strokes it should take you to play a particular hole.

PITCH—A short shot with high trajectory. Also, your fable to your spouse to get out of family obligations and onto the course.

PITCH AND RUN—A short shot followed immediately by nature's call to the bushes.

PUTT—The green strokes in which you watch your ball avoid falling into the cup.

PUTTER—The one club you can use in your office or den.

ROUGH—Home to most golfers.

RUN—The distance the ball rolls after hitting the ground, or what you do after your ball strikes another golfer.

SCRATCH PLAYER—Someone with a zero handicap whom you should not wager against, or a player who hits into poison oak.

SHAFT—An old Isaac Hayes movie.

SLICE—A ball that, in flight, decides to take a left turn despite your pleas for it not to.

STROKE PLAY—Competition based on total scores designed to save you embarrassment and possible loss of money until the end of the game.

SUDDEN DEATH—Playing in a severe lightning storm.

TOP—Hitting the top half of the ball because you looked up to see where it went before hitting it. Common.

TOUCHDOWN—Wrong sport.

UNDERCLUBBING—A pathetic shot that barely goes beyond your shadow.

UNPLAYABLE LIE—When your ball lands inside a hollow tree.

WATER HAZARD—Any stream, lake, pond, river, sea, brook, ocean, drinking fountain, toilet, or birdbath in which your ball can land with a splash.

WEDGE—Used for getting a ball out of a hazard.

WEDGIE—What's happened to your shorts by the 15th hole.

The Top 10 Reasons for the Popularity of Golf

A COUNTDOWN

10. You get to play on manicured grass that you were yelled at for walking on as a youngster.
9. The PGA doesn't go on strike.
8. Nobody does "The Wave."
7. There's no DiamondVision scoreboard with commercials.
6. Those carts are damn fun to drive.
5. It's hard not to like a guy named Fuzzy.
4. You have an excuse to be out of the house before anyone else is even awake.
3. It's a sport you can play better at than most Presidents (and Vice Presidents) of the United States.
2. Howard Cosell doesn't broadcast it.
1. You can wear clothes that don't match and nobody minds.

The Weekend Golfer— A Case Study

It's a balmy spring night, and Dr. Ira Weitzman and his wife, Muriel, are visiting their friends Chad and Gladys Cornwald. As the clock nears midnight, Ira's subtle glances at his digital Rolex become more frequent. Ira is anxious to get a good night's sleep prior to his 6 A.M. tee-off time. While the ladies continue their conversation, Ira's hands are now forming a grip. Concentrating on a small fuzzball resting atop the white shag rug, he practices a short imaginary putt. The fuzzball remains in place, but the doctor's actions attract the eye of Gladys, the bewildered hostess. "I'm glad my vacuum cleaner doesn't leave more fuzzballs," she jokes. "Otherwise I could open a miniature golf course." Muriel hides her embarrassment by adding, "He's impossible. When it comes to golf, I play second fiddle. He even brought his caddie on our honeymoon."

The levity continues as Chad joins in, joking about his own game. "I've been forced to let people play through on the driving range."

Ira begins to enjoy the conversation. Soon he's foaming at the mouth, eager to talk about the back nine at the club or perhaps for a brief chat about the new solar-powered carts. He realizes, however, that this is not the proper time or place to discuss "The Game." His mind is now wandering back to last Sunday's chip shot from the sand trap onto the green on the always difficult 16th hole. Ira's daydream is abruptly halted when he hears his wife suggest that Chad fill the vacancy in tomorrow's foursome. (It so happened that Ira's usual partner, Dr. Meltzer, lost a domestic dispute concerning his attendance at his daughter's wedding that particular afternoon.) Instantly, thoughts of coal for Christmas, a power failure during the Super Bowl, and other major disappointments fill Ira's head. How can Chad be included in an experience which rivals that of being stranded at sea with Cheryl Tiegs, Loni Anderson, and two cases of Michelob? Chad and golf simply don't paint a pretty picture.

The ride home provides a tense silence for the Weitzmans. Muriel finally breaks the silence by cautiously asking the obvious question: "What's wrong with Chad joining you tomorrow morning?" Ira considers the question carefully before answering. Could his wife be getting even with him for some previous "misunderstandings"? Perhaps the question is just another subtle reminder that he failed to attend his niece's piano recital in order to meet Arnold Palmer at the opening of a local sporting goods store. Perhaps she was retaliating for the time he kept her family waiting three hours for Thanksgiving dinner while shooting a horrendous 23 over par.

Ira then proceeds to explain what it would mean to have Chad playing with him the following morning. Chad will not only slow down the game, but he'll discuss things like home decorating and his kid's poor grades in algebra while approaching the green. He'll spend twenty minutes looking for a ball, while constantly complaining that someone else must have picked it up. Chad will not only improve the lie of his ball, but will probably use a tee in the sand trap. He'll do all of this while continuing a running commentary on how and why he should do this more often, how wonderful the grass smells, and how great it is to do a lot of walking. Ira finally draws a good analogy, explaining that Chad's presence on the course will be tantamount to including their neighbor's sheepdog, Ozzy, in Muriel's weekly bridge game. Muriel, still not completely understanding the importance of "the right foursome," simply replies, "Well, it's better than playing with a stranger." To this Ira responds, "Not exactly. You can lose a stranger in a water hazard if you're lucky, but Chad knows how to swim." They remain silent during the rest of the ride, and they have mutual "headaches" at bedtime.

The following day brings a more peaceful quiet to the Weitzman household as the rain falls gently against the windows, in the yard—and on the course. Ira, awake at 5 A.M., promptly returns to sleep, with dreams of watching "The Bob Hope Classic" that afternoon dancing in his head. Within minutes the phone rings. Muriel groggily reaches up and answers it—it's Chad, confirming that the game has been canceled. Muriel, aware of her husband's return to bed, tells Chad that the game is indeed off. Ira, with a smile on his face, breathes a sigh of relief. Muriel, unaware of Ira's afternoon rendezvous with Bob Hope and NBC Sports, invites Chad and Gladys over . . . to spend the entire afternoon!

The Five-Year-Old Golfer

HOW TO DETECT A FUTURE JACK NICKLAUS

Are you raising a future golf enthusiast? You may want to nurture those budding skills from an early age.

Here are some questions to ask yourself when determining if you've got a future tour player in your nest.

Does your boy or girl . . .

1. Enjoy wearing bright-colored pants?
2. Frequently misspell the word *tea* on spelling exams?
3. Write homework assignments with a tiny pencil?
4. Have another kid carrying his or her schoolbooks?
5. Have posters of Orville Moody on the wall?
6. Yell "FORE!" during dodgeball?
7. Whisper while watching any sporting event?
8. Have trouble counting past eighteen?
9. Insult neighborhood kids by calling them "Duffers" and "Hackers"?
10. Refer to bed-wetting as casual water?

These are all early signs of a future golfer.

Pars for the Course

Golf courses generally have three types of holes: difficult, more difficult, and "Are you kidding?" To simplify matters the golf powers that be created the simple system of designating holes as either par 3, par 4, or par 5.

The following personality guide illustrates exactly what type of golfer enjoys playing each type of hole.

PAR-3 HOLES— UP TO 250 YARDS

This is your opportunity to use the wrong iron simply to show how well you've strengthened those biceps at the gym. No matter how much you spoil your chance for par you can still enjoy the thrill of clearing the green by some 30 yards. For those of you who understand the meaning of the word *finesse*, this is your chance to ever so casually, and with the perfect trajectory, pop one into a nearby water hazard or sand trap.

Par-3 lovers are the same people who never cook with anything but their microwave, drive a compact car, leave a baseball game in the seventh inning, and won't rent a movie that's longer than 90 minutes.

PAR-4 HOLES— UP TO 470 YARDS

This covers most holes, most courses, but not most golfers' scores. Because a par 4 is so common, one should expect the unexpected. Hazards, hills, bunkers, doglegs, trees, grazing cows, perhaps a venomous snake or two are all ways in which the creators of the course like to spice up these common golf holes.

The object is to reach the green on two strokes and a kick, and putt it in in one stroke and an exaggerated (2-foot) gimme.

Because they're so common, a par-4 lover is the "Average Joe" with 2.5 kids, a midsize car, a mortgage, and a few extra pounds to shed around the waist.

PAR-5 HOLES— NO MAXIMUM

The ultimate test of your eyesight, the par 5 is laid out to make golfers say, "I told you we should have rented an electric cart." Basically designed to get rid of duffers and hackers, these holes can, and often do, go on forever. Playing a par 5 can last longer than the average Hollywood marriage.

Par-5 lovers are the same people who still drive gas guzzlers, watch an entire 12-part mini-series, vacation in the great outdoors, and like three-and-a-half-hour football games.

Most avid players love the game, love the course, but hate whatever the par is, unless of course they get it.

20 Things God Created *Just* to Make Your Life Difficult

1. Wind
2. Rain
3. Rough
4. Insects
5. Uphill lies
6. Downhill lies
7. HILLS!
8. Trees
9. Branches
10. The Pacific Ocean
11. The Atlantic Ocean
12. Sundays
13. Professional golfers
14. 6 A.M.
15. Sand
16. Bodies of water
17. Cliffs
18. Rocks
19. Bright sunlight
20. The notion of "playing golf"

2nd HOLE—

Golf Through the Ages

If you watch the game, it's fun. If you play it, it's recreation. If you work at it, it's golf.

—*Bob Hope*

The Origins of the Game

THE HISTORY OF GOLF

The word *golf* is derived from the Germanic word *Kolbe*, which means simply, "I can't even see the flag."

The game is either Scottish or Dutch in origin; there have been arguments for both. Dutch Masters (the old gentlemen with the cigars) painted many pictures of people playing a game resembling golf, or hockey. The stick-like object and the way in which the figures are standing resemble golf. The two men beating each other senseless in the background, however, suggests hockey.

It was the Scottish who first played a game, six centuries ago, whereby they attempted to hit a ball cross-country without any form of defense by an opponent. Continuously hitting the stationary ball gave the Scottish men an opportunity to get farther and father away from their wives, which is also true of golf as many men know it today.

The idea of getting the ball into a hole originated quite by accident. It seems one participant put down a cup of ale and another cross-country "golfer" landed his ball in it. This also established the idea for the first ale hazard, which was transformed to water hazard less than a century later.

The first actual planned course was the entire country of Wales, par 937. However, the residents of Wales complained about balls destroying their homes and frightening their livestock. Thus a smaller, more manageable course was established.

The ball, which had been the size of a baseball, was changed during wartime in Europe to save on the expense of manufacturing such large balls. Also, the golfing community began favoring the round ball over the square wooden balls being made in Holland. For a time the small, more golflike ball was made out of rubber, cork, acorns, and was covered with feathers. After several years of mistaking golf balls for birds and vice versa, the feathers were used on the inside of the ball. The ball changed several more times over the years. The two-piece ball was made in two separate halves, whereas the three-piece ball added a vest. Dimples were added to the ball in the late 1880s so that players waiting to tee off could try to balance one ball on top of the other. Many companies created their own balls, including Hershey, which manufactured the chocolate golf ball, abandoned after just one tournament because it melted by the 12th hole.

The idea of playing 18 holes as opposed to 6, 12, or 31 originated in the 1700s. The Society of St. Andrews Golfers in Scotland had a course of 11 holes, which they played once forward and once backward, thus giving them a 22-hole round. It seemed that two of the holes, however, were too close to the nearby moors, and the surrounding quicksand was causing the then customary eightsome to lose an average of half its members. The Society sold the two hazardous holes to France and had a remaining 9-hole course, which, when played twice, gave them 18 holes. While the Society attempted to purchase more stable land to replace the two lost holes, a shrewd tavern owner opened a small inn just off the course and called it The Nineteenth Hole. Having taken a liking to the tavern, the committee therefore decided to stay with the 18-hole course.

In memory of the many golfers lost in the moors the customary eightsomes were reduced to the now familiar foursomes.

The term *caddie* is derived from the French word *cadet*, which means "Carry those, will ya?" The idea originated with Scottish nobility who used sheep to carry their clubs. Unfortunately, the animals too frequently chose the wrong club.

Originally the job of caddie was not simply to carry clubs but to clear a path for the participants to play. The links were often covered with sheep, goats, cows, spectators, fishermen, rabbits, vendors, solicitors, prostitutes, and sports agents. It was up to the caddie to find a clear path for the ensuing shot and mark the hole with the freshly plucked feather from a gull.

The animals often dug holes in the ground for safety from the players, protection from the wind, and to avoid confrontations with insurance salesmen. These holes, often filled with sand blown in from the beaches or dung left by the animals, formed the initial hazards now so important to the game.

Great Dates in Golf History

1457   Golf is discouraged by an act of British Parliament because it interferes with archery practice.

1569   The first known lady golfer, Mary Queen of Scots, requests her own beheading after 5 putting a par 3.

1665   Unknown caddie decides to put clubs in golf bag for first time. Previously clubs and bag were carried separately.

1744   The first golf club forms: The Honourable Company of Edinburgh Golfers.

1744   The first membership restrictions are imposed by The Honourable Company of Edinburgh Golfers.

1744   Membership restrictions eliminate all members of The Honourable Company of Edinburgh Golfers. Club reforms with less stringent guidelines.

1744   First Bob Hope Classic is played.

1744–59   The first rules of golf drawn up. No one pays any attention to them.

1766   Japan invents the driving range; not sure yet how it will be used.

1773   Archery is discouraged by an act of British Parliament because it interferes with golf.

1779   Golf first played in United States somewhere outside New York City because golfers have trouble finding parking spaces.

1792   Betsy Ross, having done such a great job with the flag, is commissioned to sew 18 smaller flags with numbers on them to be used for the first American golf course.

1881   First women's golf tournament organized at Musselburgh, England.

1881   Women golfers complain about not receiving the same prize money as men.

1895   The first U.S. Open is won by Horace Rawlins in Rhode Island. The relatively small course covered the entire state.

1916   The U.S. PGA is founded in New York. Members have trouble finding parking spaces.

1922   First golf event covered by radio. Listeners complain that they can't hear commentators who are whispering.

1929   Depression causes courses to be reduced to 14 holes.

1935   First Phoenix Open in Arizona is held in mere 110-degree heat. Players threaten to kill for a water hazard.

1944   First camouflage balls are sold during war.

1954   Arnold Palmer wins U.S. Amateur title—but can he make it as a pro?

1959   Asian golf circuit begins in Hong Kong. Players finish 18-hole course and within an hour are ready to play again.

1959   Elvis plays golf. Shoots a 93 in Memphis.

1962   Johnny Carson first ends monologue with golf swing.

1963   Spiro Agnew and Gerald Ford take golf lessons together. Golf instructor is struck by ball. No one warns public of future danger.

1966   First televised American coverage of a

tournament in color has millions of Americans seeing nothing but green for days.

1969   Man places flag in crater on moon, creating all-time longest first hole.

1973   Rosemary Woods caught altering Richard Nixon's golf score.

1976   First Israeli tournament course built. Long debates over borders of holes.

1979   Andy Williams Classic is first major American tournament won by someone named Fuzzy.

1980   Movie *Caddyshack* filmed.

1984   First instructional golf video released, entitled "The Three Stooges Play Augusta."

1988   David Letterman drops two golf balls from window of Rockefeller Center. Building later sold to Japanese to conduct further golf research.

1991   *Unofficial Golfer's Handbook* appears in bookstores.

3rd
HOLE—

Tools of the Trade

In golf, I'm one under. One under a tree, one under a rock, one under a bush . . .

—Gerry Cheevers,
former NHL goalie

Getting Started

Remember when you gripped your first club? Placed your first ball on a tee? Placed it there again because it rolled off? Remember your first drive and the obscenity you yelled as it struck a tree to your extreme right? Remember how, each time you took your tee shot that first day, everyone moved farther and farther away from you?

Starting out in golf isn't easy. For that matter, neither is playing after 20 years, but at least you have some marginal idea of what you're doing out there. Torturing yourself.

For those of you just taking up the great game, or trying to coax a friend or relative into playing, here are the absolute basics to getting started.

WHAT TO GET . . . AND WHY

1. A golf bag. Ladies, it's not an oblong purse, and it need not match your shoes. Guys, keep in mind that this is for carrying the clubs; it's not a clubhouse—don't plan on moving in. Choose something light enough to carry but sturdy if you expect to use a cart. Carts can be rented, so don't waste your money on one.

2. Clubs are nice. You don't really need 14 to start out with, but why not look like you know what you're doing? The full set of 14 will also give you a wide variety of clubs to hate, so you won't have to single out just one. And by the way, you put them in the bag handle first.

3. Balls will help your game. Yes, they're the little ones with the cute dimples all over them. Normally a dozen is fine. Since you have no idea where they'll go, however, and have never had the thrill of trying to see where one lands as it slices into another time zone, maybe you ought to spring for three dozen.

4. Tees. Believe it or not, when struck powerfully enough with a club, they often break, and sometimes even go off into never-never land. Thus, a bag or two is recommended. The pointy part goes into the ground.

5. A hat or a visor. No, it doesn't figure in the game, but it'll make you look like a golfer, shield you from the sun, the rain, and from others eager to get a look at the person who just dug up the first fairway.

6. A golf glove. No, you can't substitute a first baseman's mitt. A batting glove, however, often serves the purpose. Why do you think so many people attend Batting

Glove Day at the ballpark?

7. Golf shoes . . . with spikes. You can get away without real golf shoes, but it's great fun walking on the concrete from the clubhouse to the 1st tee and hearing that little clicking sound.

8. A towel. A beach towel is excessive, but a small towel will come in handy as your clubs intimately visit what's known as "The Rough" . . . or in your case "The Impossible." If you have a tendency to get sweaty palms, a towel to dry your grips will help you hang on to those 14 clubs you paid for. After all, the only thing worse than your shot going into a pond or ravine is your club following it.

9. Head covers. Not for you. You've already got a hat. These are for your woods. This will hide the incredible amount of damage you'll do to them in the first few weeks—make that months. Okay, years!

10. A book of golf rules. No one actually uses it on the course, but having it will intimidate the hell out of your opponent.

This is all you really need to get out on the links (that's another word for golf course) and start playing. You may choose not to play all 18 holes the first time out. Nine holes, however, are highly recommended over three, four, or five.

Don't worry about your score or where some of your shots land. Remember, it's every beginner's golf-given right to check out the entire landscape from sand trap to bunker, to sand trap. You paid your green fee, the acreage is yours!

Buying Clubs

The proper club can help the improper game, but what is the proper club? The right set of clubs is obviously the set that will improve your game, lower your handicap, and put your scores in the 70s. Unfortunately these clubs don't exist. There are, however, about 14,000 brands of clubs designed to help you do just about anything to one of 10,000 brands of golf balls. New models of golf clubs are designed more frequently than new models of cars. They're designed to help you hit the ball farther, harder, straighter, higher, lower, with more spin, with no spin, with topspin, with a two-step cha-cha movement, and with the proper sound for the TV microphone.

Essentially, your clubs should help your game and be rugged enough to withstand the abuse they'll get for not obliging. A few things to consider when buying a set of clubs include: the grip size, loft, length, clubface angle, the price, the manufacturer, the shaft flex, the shine, the price, the weight, the color, the price, they type of grip, the people who endorse them, how they were shipped to the store, how many days they've been for sale, the temperature in the store that's selling them, and why they're being "marked down."

Clubs aren't just bought off the rack; you must feel a sense of comfort, for these are your partners and you must relate well to each other. Sure, there are 14 of them and just one of you, but you're in command. Study each iron, make sure it feels right and is the proper length. Can you see your reflection in the clubface? When fondling the woods, are you aroused? These are questions to ask yourself—and definitely not anyone else. Does the club instill confidence when you hold it or is it crying out . . . please don't hurt me!

Clubs are designed to suit the golfer. Many golfers, however, aren't designed to suit the clubs. Many clubs are sole weighted to make lofting easier. Others are heel and toe weighted, increasing the sweet spot on the club. Now you know a little something so you won't sound totally ignorant when dealing with the salesperson.

A good golf pro shop will employ someone who not only knows the game and plays much better than you do, but will manage to include that fact into the conversation quite frequently.

They'll convince you that because they know golf, and you don't, that you should place your trust in their hands, and while you're at it, place your wallet there as well. A pro shop, however, will be able to answer your questions—usually in terms you won't completely understand. A sporting goods shop may save you money (and condescension), but you may be forced to deal with sales help that doesn't specialize in golf. If an answer to your question about loft involves the terms *high sticking* or *infield fly rule*, you're dealing with a nongolfer just anxious to make a sale.

If you've bought clubs before, or if you're buying them for the first time, here is a brief glossary of things to keep in mind:

GRIP TYPE—Rubber or leather are most common—Velcro is good if you frequently let go of the club on your follow-through. Wood is rare but good for carpenters or anyone who thinks getting a splinter or two is macho.

METAL OR WOOD WOODS?—If you're a purist who uses a wooden tennis racket and doesn't think Wrigley Field should have gotten lights, then use wood heads on your woods. If you're trendy, use an aluminum tennis racket, know that aluminum bats would hit baseballs into neighboring states and ruin the game, like things that are shiny, and wouldn't mind a little added power, you should try metal woods, even if the term *metal woods* is an oxymoron.

THE SHAFT FLEX—This is how much the shaft gives, or bends. Contrary to most sex handbooks you may not always want a stiff shaft. However, you generally don't want a shaft that can be knotted in the middle either.

WEIGHT OF THE CLUB—Simple rule of thumb: If it takes more than one person to swing it, it's too heavy for you.

When buying a previously owned (used) set of clubs it's a good idea to inquire whether any of the clubs have ever been struck by lightning. Preferably they have been, thus greatly reducing the odds of them being struck again.

WHICH CLUB TO USE?

You're in the rough, but your lie isn't bad. In front of you are two trees and a hill leading up to the green (which you can't see). You're about 125 yards away and a slight wind is blowing in your face. It's drizzling and your nose is running. Your partner, a business associate who is grossly overpaid for the job he does, is on top of the hill looking down, waiting for you to hit. He's impatient as always. What club do you use?

1. You can take your basic wedge shot, popping the ball over your obnoxious partner and onto the green.
2. You can take a 6 iron and, hit just right, it'll graze your partner, slowing it down so it won't travel a mile past the green.
3. You can ask your partner's advice, hit badly, and blame him for the rest of the day.

You're teeing off on a 156-yard par 3 over a lake, with three bunkers in front of a small green. The wind is behind you, but luck hasn't been. Behind the green are several large oak trees. To the right of the lake is a tool shed and the cart path. You have three options.

1. You can use a 7 iron and a prayer and try to clear the lake.
2. You can try banking a 6 iron off an oak.
3. You can try lining a 3 iron off the shed, hoping it will roll along the cart path and end up near the green.

How Well Do You Know Your Golf Balls?

Besides your club, your golf balls are your only allies when

Name That Club—A Quiz

You probably refer to each club other than your putter by its number. But, do you know the correct names for your clubs? Here's a little quiz.

1. The real name for the 2 wood is:
   A. "That Darn Club I Hate"
   B. "The Wilbur Wood"
   C. "The Natalie Wood"
   D. "The Brassie"

2. The correct name for a 5 iron is:
   A. "Masher"
   B. "Mashie"
   C. "Murray"

3. The spot on the club that you want to strike the ball with is called:
   A. "The Sweet Spot" because the ball travels so nicely
   B. "The G Spot" because you can't find it
   C. "The Liver Spot" because your club is getting old

4. A niblick is another name for:
   A. Your partner
   B. A golfer with a small appetite
   C. A 9 iron

5. The 2 iron is also known as:
   A. The mid-iron
   B. The flat iron
   C. The club showoffs use off the tee on a 490-yard hole to embarrass you

---

facing 7,200 yards of wind, hilly terrain, rough underbrush, dense trees, and your scorecard. Therefore it's very important to know your balls well when venturing onto the links. With so many different brands on the market, it's crucial to zero in on the ball that's right for you. These are the questions today's golfers are now asking themselves about the balls they're using.

Does your ball have more lift than drag?

Does your ball drop in a steep arc?

Does your ball drop whenever it's over water?

Can your ball land and stick like Velcro to the green?

How many dimples does your ball have?

Do the dimples on your ball spell out the word *HELP*?

Are your balls allergic to the sweet spot on your clubface?

Does a 20-mph wind generally have you ducking your own ball on its return flight?

Does your ball have bite, or does it run like someone bit it?

Is your ball covered with Surlyn, a similar covering, or papier-mâché?

If you back a station wagon over your ball, is it damaged?

Does your ball land gently on the fairway or dig itself a tunnel to hide in?

Does your ball have a brand name on it or does it say "Bernie's Budget Balls #3"?

Has your brand of ball been outlawed in 16 states?

Does your ball listen to you?

In the Bag

WHAT TO KEEP IN THE GOLF BAG

1. Your clubs.
2. Various balls. Good ones for those holes where wooded areas and water hazards aren't prevalent. X'ed out or range balls for those holes where your confidence level sinks just as your ball will into the water. One with a dirty word on it to get a chuckle out of your partner, and a few with the exact name and number that the others in your foursome usually play. This is so that if you're both looking for a ball in the woods or the rough, you can claim yours is the one with the better lie—it's basically lying about the lie.
3. Tees and tiny pencils. It's also nice to have an eraser on one of those pencils in case you manage to convince someone that your shank on the 3rd hole was really due to some imaginary car horn.
4. A towel and/or cloth are nice for cleaning your clubs, your hands, and stuffing in the mouth of anyone giving unwanted advice.
5. A cellular phone is a new addition to the golf bag. It's great to be able to call ahead and reserve a table at the Nineteenth Hole. It might also serve to inform those back home that you're in a sudden-death playoff and won't be there to greet the in-laws. Dialing the weather forecast might also help you pick up or slow down your pace, depending on whether or not you're hoping the match gets rained out.

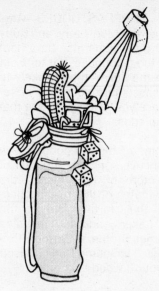

6. An umbrella is a good idea, especially one that's designed to hook on to your cart. An umbrella with a little flagstick on the top is always a good practical joke for those teeing off behind you.

7. A change of clothing. It's a plus to be able to walk into the clubhouse after the match and not let on that you've been through muck and mud in your day on the links. Many a seasoned golfer can smell a 95 walking in, so cologne or perfume is also a nice touch. If you're trying to impress a client, you might opt for a chlorine-scented cologne so that he or she will think you own your own swimming pool or are a regular member at the country club.

8. Airline-sized bottles of booze can improve a bad day provided they don't rattle around too much in your bag.

9. A small radio, Walkman, or portable TV can make you an invaluable member of the foursome. Your score will be secondary to your important updates on the football or baseball scores.

10. A travel magazine or brochure is a nice touch when playing with someone you want to impress. "Yep, this course in Rio last month was a real killer . . . and did I show you where I played on my recent trip to Maui?"

11. A tiny tool kit is a good idea for tightening clubheads, shutting off sprinklers, or futilely attempting to fix a water fountain.

12. Toilet paper. Can't hurt.

Other items that have been found in golf bags include good luck charms, discarded cellophane from the last 32 times new golf balls were opened, a compass, suntan lotion, snack foods, a leg of lamb, a portable fax machine, condoms, Nintendo games, a wash-and-wear tuxedo for dinner, radar equipment for ball hunting, a video entitled "Golf According to W. C. Fields," fuzzy dice from the rearview mirror of a '57 Chevy, a curling iron, a dozen water balloons, a Spiro T. Agnew hand puppet, and a signed prenuptial marriage agreement detailing who gets to continue playing at the club.

Head Covers

You can tell a lot about golfers by what they cover their clubheads with. Once upon a time there wasn't much choice, but today you can have any number of designs or characters adorning the head of your club and keeping your woods warm. But what does it all mean?

Here are some to look out for:

THE SEVEN DWARFS OR DISNEY HEAD COVERS—This is not someone who's going to take the game seriously. Beware when they start whipping out the Disney World photos while you're waiting to tee off.

HAND-SEWN COVERS BY MOM—This is carrying the old Oedipus complex a bit too far. This is a mamma's-boy golfer who'll probably need help handling the rake at the sand traps and will spend an inordinate amount of time keeping his ball clean.

KITTEN COVERS—Any lady with kittens on her woods can't really be a golfer. She's got a zest for the outdoors and is likely to spend all day puttering around the course—and feeding the ducks.

THE THREE STOOGES—Anyone with Moe, Larry, and Curly on their clubs may be a hoot in the clubhouse, but look out on the links—they're likely to disassemble your cart or replace your 9 iron with one that explodes.

Some of today's popular new head covers include the cast of "Phantom of the Opera," the "Playmates of the Year" collection, the starting five of the L.A. Lakers, and the amusing "Warner Brother's Cartoon Collection," including Bugs himself for your 3 wood.

Headgear

Visors must be white—it's the law. A good visor protects you from the sun and shields you from having to look at taller golfers. It's a nice touch to have an adjustable visor for those days on which you get a haircut or a swelled head. But what should your visor say in the front? Nothing is always classy, but a couple hundred advertising companies would prefer that you wear one bearing a product name. You might therefore call this an "Ad-Visor."

It's important that a visor not pop up each time you mistakenly pick your head up, or do a complete 360-degree turn on your backswing. But even if you find a visor that doesn't budge, it's essential to your game to tug on it often. After all, the primary use for a visor is to have something else to adjust prior to your shot.

Golf hats vary more than visors. The little air-ventilated cap is convenient to let the top of your head breathe, or if you're having a "rough" day, let it hyperventilate. These caps are machine washable, which means toss it in any machine, including the dishwasher or blender, and it'll come out fine. In fact, these basic golf caps often outlast your clubs, your bag, your marriage, and your desire to play anymore. They're also ideal if you ever choose to drive a taxi. If you get the terry-cloth kind, it can double as a hand towel. Just wipe your hands or clubface off on the top of your head.

If you're not into caps, how about a white bucket hat? This gives you the "I don't play other sports and really am not very athletic" look. They're light, comfortable, and easy to throw after landing in a bunker. These hats are also ideal when used to search for balls in water hazards, and they dry out in a couple of days. Another plus about the bucket hat is that no matter what you do to it, it'll retain its shape—which wasn't much to start with. They're also good for feeding horses.

There's always the "tailored hat," which often says, "Look at my hat, not my game." Feathers are nice provided a bird doesn't choose your hat to nest in. To avoid having this hat blow off on every third fairway, it's advisable either to tie it on or staple it to your head.

How about the straw hat? With a nice colorful band around it, a straw hat can enhance that macho image in men, and give that "I don't want anyone to see me out here" look to the ladies. Because straw hats are designed not to stay on your head, they're not adjustable or washable, and it's a good idea not to get "too attached" to one.

The main things to remember when buying golf headgear is that it should not have earflaps, should not weigh 3 to 5 pounds, and should generally look like something you wouldn't wear anyplace but on the golf course. It's also advisable to avoid hats with propellers on top, brims that glow in the dark or squirt water, or pitch helmets.

19 Things to Do with an Old Golf Club

1. Make an odd-looking umbrella.
2. Use an iron at the fireplace as a poker.
3. Make your own CB antenna.
4. Prod cattle.
5. Prod coworkers.
6. Take four 3 woods and build a low canopy on your bed.

7. Mark off that proposed garden you'll never get around to planting.

8. Reach that ball stuck on the screen behind home plate at the ballpark.

9. Use that wood you always hated for a rather pathetic speed bump in the driveway.

10. Use a 2 iron as a short but powerful hockey stick—with good lift to your slapshot.

11. Use a wedge and make a long shoehorn.

12. How about a walking stick?

13. Put a lightning rod on the doghouse of your neighbor's pit bull.

14. Give a basketball player a backscratcher.

15. Give your lawn jockey something to hold.

16. Sharpen one end and pick up junk on the beach.

17. Use your 9 iron or wedge to slide chips off the roulette table.

18. Make a set of odd-looking, ineffective windshield wipers for an 18 wheeler.

19. Attach little plastic men, lay eight clubs across a wooden box, and build a Foosball game.

Added Equipment

For the golfer who carefully reads those instruction books that discuss aiming the clubface, placing body weight, and other tricks of the trade, here are a few other things you might need on the course to enter the serious realm of a "par" golfer.

An odometer or yardage counter so you can gauge the precise difference between 190 and 160 yards to the green.

Blinders so you can see only where you're aiming and none of the surrounding hazards.

A carpenter's leveler to place on your shoulders to keep you properly positioned at address—especially on the slopes. Good for reading the greens, too.

A weather vane to keep you and the wind in sync at all times.

A bathroom scale to keep the right percentage of weight on the proper foot.

A lead-rimmed cap or visor to keep your head down while you swing.

A geometric compass and protractor to make sure the clubface is open the proper amount at the address.

A washable V-neck sweater to wear at all times on the course to know exactly where your feet are placed in conjunction with the ball.

A telescopic viewfinder to make sure you can always see the flagstick and have it lined up correctly.

Advanced Equipment

The more avid a golfer you become, the more you'll want every golf-related item you can get your hands on—and boy are they out there on the market!! It's astounding what you can buy if you look hard enough. For a mere $70 you can lighten your golf bag considerably by carrying a club with an adjustable head that changes from a putter to a wedge just by turning a screw. Yes, it's 17 clubs in one! Yes, people will laugh at you on the course as you spend your day adjusting and readjusting your clubface from 7 iron to 5 iron to 9 iron. But if it's golf items you want, there's more. How about a collapsible putter that you can fold up and put in your pocket? It does exist, and it's practical for sneaking into the office for a little afternoon practice.

Have trouble with your grip? There's now a spray available for your grips that prevents the club from slipping. So what if it takes two fellow golfers to pry the club from your hand! You want more? How about the ultimate? Neon shafts. Sun going down? Cloudy day? Play by the glow of your clubs. A dozen illuminated colors. They're on the market.

Buying added equipment can be fun, but remember to read the fine print. Here are some things you may want to keep in mind:

1. Never buy golf shoes with a warning sticker—"Don't get them wet."
2. Avoid adjustable golf shoes—"One size fits all."
3. Be wary of any club with easy "snap-on" grips.
4. Never buy irons with the heads made of steel wool.
5. Be cautious of any complete set, clubs and bag, for only $19.95.
6. Never buy a putter from a guy selling clubs in the woods just off the 12th fairway.
7. Try to avoid using any balls with pictures of Moe, Larry, or Curly on them.
8. Never buy an automatic score-keeping device that doesn't register under 100.
9. If a club-cleaning kit contains dangerous explosives, it might not be for you.
10. Never buy a 9 iron/umbrella combo.
11. Never buy previously used tees.
12. When shopping for a golf glove, don't let anyone con you into buying Snoopy golf mittens.
13. Don't be fooled by a golf cart advertisement that claims 0 to 60 in 6.3 seconds. You'll rarely have a chance to test it out.
14. Never buy a set of clubs from a guy on a street corner selling velvet paintings of Jack Nicklaus shaking hands with Elvis.

15. Try to refrain from buying a $2.99 automatic green reading machine.
16. At no time should you ever even consider buying a combination indoor putting machine/outdoor barbecue.
17. Never buy golf shoes with little fuzzy balls as tassels.
18. Never buy golf balls with fuzzy little shoes drawn on them.
19. Don't buy a golf bag that weighs more than you do.
20. Never buy head covers that smell remarkably like old sweat socks.

Don't say we didn't warn you!

Fun Accessories

Here are a few new items to look for . . .

STRINGER BALLS

These new golf balls are ideal for beginners. They have a very thin white string that unravels as the ball flies off in some undesired direction. The end of the string should be tied to your cleats so that you can follow the string all the way to your ball. The ball, with string wrapped around it, however, weighs an

additional 21 ounces, and the string is only 120 yards long. These problems are being worked on to create this easy method of finding your ball.

THE AUTOMATIC BALL REMOVER

Tired of bending down to pull your ball from the cup? Have trouble finding balls deep down in the bag? The Automatic Ball Remover uses just the precise amount of suction to pull your ball from the hole or the bag, and with an adjustable handle (up to 4 feet long) you'll never again have to bend to pick up a ball. It is highly recommended that this suction device not be used for other purposes.

THE NEW 17 IRON

The manufacturers of the 17 iron are all set to market this new club for those who either overshoot the green or are anxious to get back to the clubhouse. The clubface is designed to hit the ball with the precise trajectory to land 50 to 100 yards behind you. This club might also be utilized in situations where the ball is resting against a tree or another such obstacle, whereby hitting it backward might help your game, or injure your opponents, who will have no idea where to stand whenever you grab your 17 iron.

FLAT-TOP TEES

What fun you can have slipping them into a friend's golf bag and watching as he or she tries to tee up, but can't get the ball to stay on the tee. It's almost as much fun as the Peeing Putter, which, when gripped tightly, squirts a pool of casual water around the ball before you get to putt. Who said golfers don't appreciate a good joke now and then?

THE TWO-BALL POP-UP TEE

Slice that first shot into the woods? The new Two-Ball Pop-Up Tee acts like an automatic driving range, because it slips a second ball onto the tee. Take another shot! Everyone will let you because they're so impressed by the new tee-off device. All you need are the balls to use it.

THE SOLAR-POWERED CART

This invention actually hit the course back in the early 1980s, but was recalled when foursomes complained about very slow rides between holes on overcast days. In fact, at one country club, players had to push the carts out from a tunnel connecting the front and back nine. The new solar-powered carts store up energy and, when left in the tropical sun of Florida or Hawaii for extended periods of time, have been known to do 0 to 60 in just 3.4 seconds. The carts, complete with safety belts and racing stripes are, unfortunately, hard to stop and overshoot most balls by a good 40 to 50 yards.

THE ELECTRIC PENCIL

Tired of losing those little pencils? The electric pencil can always be found. As soon as you bend over to pull your ball from the cup this little 9-volt pencil will remind you abruptly with a mini-electric shock that it's somewhere on your person. The pencil will also emit a shock if you attempt to put in an incorrect score for the hole, which thus far has made it a relatively unpopular item. If lost somewhere in your golf bag, it will burst into flames within 30 seconds.

THE INFLATABLE TEE TENT

Good for the putting green as well, this little three-sided tent can be inflated in less than 30 seconds and will shield the entire foursome from the elements while teeing off or putting. It's also great for hiding snacks, beer, or anything else from grounds keepers. The tent, which comes in nine shades of green, is strong enough to withstand chip shots from the foursome behind you as you party on the green. For newlyweds, there's a fourth flap that can be closed if necessary.

THE POLO IRON

This specially made iron is for those who want to add excitement to their game by striking the ball from a moving golf cart, polo style. The sturdy club is designed to hit for distance, power, and from a cart traveling at speeds up to 40 mph.

THE INFLATABLE CADDIE

Don't have a caddie? Want people to think you do? Buy the inflatable caddie. Just blow it up and it stands there holding out a club for you to take. At 5 feet 4 inches tall, the inflatable caddie looks like you've hand picked this lad from the golfing academy. The best part is that you can vent your anger without getting real blood on your clubs. He's easy to work with, easy to inflate, and some golfers may even enjoy blowing him up! Tired of your caddie? Pack him up in your old golf bag until next time.

THE MEXICAN JUMPING COIN

Designed to utilize the same principle as a Mexican jumping bean, the Mexican Jumping Coin is ideal for marking your ball on the green. This little baby is designed to jump ever so slightly toward the cup. Thus, while you stand quietly by, watching your opponent line up his or her putt, your marker will be making your 10-foot putt a good 2 feet closer, and chances are no one will notice. Of course, you must face the jumping coin in the right direction or your 10 footer could turn out to be a 14-foot putt.

Five Things a Golfer Wants from a Caddie

1. A caddie should be willing to throw himself or herself on a ball cascading into a lateral water hazard.
2. A caddie should be ready to get on a plane and accompany the golfer anywhere in the world at anytime.
3. A caddie should have no recognizable social life.
4. An adolescent caddie should be neutered.
5. A caddie should not have hayfever!

Five Things a Caddie Wants from a Golfer

1. A golfer should be able to take full responsibility for his or her own actions, ideas, and game strategy. Or lack thereof.
2. A golfer should not expect a caddie to accompany him or her into a rest room.
3. A golfer should be expected to know when his or her outfit looks ridiculous and be willing to accept the resulting laughter.
4. A golfer should not only pay a caddie, but should remember holiday tips, pay time and a half for sudden death playoffs, and include the caddie in the will.
5. A golfer who enjoys "caddie bashing" should be dragged through the back nine by an electric cart.

Shopping for a Caddie

Caddying is a noble profession that began with the use of the children of nobility who carried the clubs for royalty in Europe. Today, however, few people actually use caddies other than in tournaments, and there are few professional caddying academies where the young caddies and future golfers can hone their carrying skills. Nevertheless, the caddie who hands you a 7 iron when you're still 212 yards from the green is either inexperienced or honestly believes you are Superman—or Superwoman.

Here is a short quiz to see if you know what to look for when seeking the perfect caddie.

1. The ideal caddie should:
   A. Know something about the game of golf
   B. Know little about the minimum wage
   C. Admire and revere you
   D. Be all of the above

2. Besides handing you the appropriate club, a good caddie will:
   A. Keep the equipment clean
   B. Know karate in case anyone interferes with your game
   C. Cheat in your favor
   D. Perform all of the above

3. A caddie is your:
   A. Assistant on the course
   B. Slave
   C. Scapegoat

4. A loyal caddie should:
   A. Leave at the sight of a storm cloud
   B. Help you speed up your game because of impending rain
   C. Offer to hold the umbrella in a lightning storm

5. You should not let your son or daughter caddie for you because:
   A. Your partner's dirty jokes will embarrass you
   B. Your game will embarrass you
   C. Your son or daughter will blackmail you forever

6. Your caddie should be privy to all information pertaining to:
   A. Your golf game and score
   B. Your boss, coworkers, clients, and other business associates
   C. Who you scored with on your recent "business" trip

Carts versus Feet

**To walk around the course or to ride, the great debate.
Here are the arguments for both sides.**

WALKING	RIDING
It's good exercise	Speeds up the game
You can appreciate nature	Keep cleats cleaner
More time to think about your next shot	Less time to dwell over your last shot
The way golf "was meant to be played"	Utilizes modern golf technology
Carrying a full bag gives you an excuse for hitting badly late in the round due to fatigue	Riding can make you feel lethargic, giving you an excuse for weak shots
Keeps you out of the house a lot longer	Gets you back to your pals in the clubhouse faster
Gives you more time to firm up that business deal	Allows you to spend less time entertaining your client, "The Hacker"
Gives you more time to snack between shots	Keeps the weight off because you have less time to snack between shots
Works off those extra pounds you gained going out for dinner Saturday night	

Golf on Tape

Here are some of the latest golf videos available to the public.

ANDY ROONEY ON GOLF: Ever notice how golf balls have those little dimples all over them? Thoughtful, if not totally meaningless analysis of facets of the game that no one has much interest in.

THE MICHAEL JORDAN GOLF VIDEO: How to slam dunk a putter into a moving cart! How to hurdle a water hazard! The art of sound defense!

KIDS ARE GOLFERS TOO: A fun-filled instructional romp around the course with Pee Wee Herman and Mr. Rogers. Can you spell "duffer"?

GOLFERSIZE: Jane Fonda instructs on how to stay fit between shots. How many leg lifts can you do while your partner lines up her putt?

INSIDE JACK NICKLAUS: A look at his kidneys, his liver, his pancreas, and other things inside Jack.

BUDGET GOLF: How to play the best courses in the world on less than $3.00 a day! Learn how to pose as a grounds keeper, how to fish the best balls from a water hazard, how to hot-wire a golf cart! You'll even learn the art of extorting money in damages by pretending you've been struck by a ball!

Food for Golf

BREAKFAST

Golfers like eggs, maybe because prior to their final (cooked) preparation they're the closest thing resembling a golf ball at 6 A.M. Fruit juice, tea, and cereal are good for starting the day off. Wheaties might even help psych you up mentally. Yogurt, although healthy, promotes a "far less than aggressive swing." Coffee might shake up your putting ever so slightly. However, a couple sips to keep you awake until tee-off time might not hurt. Fried foods will remind your stomach, around the 3rd or 4th hole, that perhaps you should have gone with the soft-boiled eggs.

LUNCH

It depends on two things: (1) Are you going to continue playing? (2) How are you doing? If you're going to play more holes and you're doing well, have something light like a sandwich, so you can get back out there quickly. If you're playing poorly, but plan to continue, go with burgers, fries, and junk food.

This way you can blame the rest of your bad day on being "too full from lunch." If you're finished for the day, eat whatever you want. After all, you did all that walking, took all those swings, and got all that fresh air, and that's as much "fitness" as your body ever needs.

DINNER

Avoid too much red meat—it has nothing to do with golf, but you should do so anyway. Other than that, you're on your own.

4th HOLE—

On the Course

Golf is a walk in the park ruined.

—*Mark Twain*

A Variety of Duffers

TYPES OF GOLFERS

Front nine or back nine, you're likely to run into these characters of the game. So look for them in your foursome.

THE DEFENSIVE GOLFER

True, there isn't a lot of defense in the game of golf, but the defensive golfer is defending against anything that could go wrong. Four shots around a water hazard are better than trying to go over it. Puttering along, this is the player who even goes around the windmill when playing miniature golf with the kids. Defensive golfers never lose a ball. How could they? They'll only hit it where they can see it and practically touch it. Their motto is rather play it safe than sorry, no matter how long it takes.

THE DAREDEVIL

The opposite of the defensive golfer is the daredevil. The Evil Knevil of the course, these players will dangle 95 feet from a rope to recover a shot that sliced into a nearby canyon. If there are trees, they'll clear 'em, if there's a lake, no problem, a mountain—piece of cake! The dare-devil can make an ordinary 165-yard par 3 exciting by ricocheting the ball off the nearby clubhouse. Who says golf isn't dangerous? And whatever you do don't let them drive the cart!

THE MOANER

A difficult member of any four-some, the moaner always hit better last time out. The moaner will blame the wind, the course, the grounds crew, the landscaping, breakfast, their spouse, and Dan Rather for their poor performance. Since the balls, the flags, the greens, and everything else just "isn't right," one can only wonder why the moaner bothers to play out the round. It's simple—there's nothing to do at home, the in-laws are coming over, the car isn't running well, there's nothing good on television . . .

THE CHEATER

How do four chip shots become three? Why does this player's ball always have a good lie? These are questions opponents want answered. The cheater is ready to "forget" a rule at a moment's notice. They'll take every inch you give them, and several you don't. Good cheaters know how to move a ball surreptitiously with their cleats, change a five to a four, and even find a ball that went into the woods and "just happened" to come

back out near the fairway—
"must have hit a tree."

THE LOOKER

The looker has the latest in golf
apparel, expensive new clubs,
the best-looking golf bag on
course, and a cap hand picked
by Arnold Palmer. This is the
fashion plate of any course, with
gold-plated tees and shining
spikes. The looker is determined
to impress, that is until he or she
actually tees off.

THE AUTHORITY

From your stance to your clubs,
the authority knows what you're
doing wrong. If you hit a wound
ball it should be a two piece, if
you use a 3 iron you should have
used a 4. If you do well it's ter-
rific, but listen to the authority
and you'll knock five strokes off
your game—or his or her head
off, whichever comes first. This is
the golfer who seems to be the
"know it all" of the course, every
course. Even if they've never
played those links before or
seen your game, these individ-
uals have read it all and seen it
all, and are going to tell all if you
let them.

THE POWER HITTER

The power hitter is usually the
golfer who lifts weights, and it
shows on excessively long tee

shots. It doesn't matter if it
hooks or slices, as long as the
power hitter can outdistance
you. An explosion shot out of the
sand trap looks more like someone struck a land mine, whereas
the short game is really salugi
with the green until they somehow top a power shot that rolls
onto the green. Because this is
a weight lifter it's only a cautious few who'll remind the
power hitter that golf is a game
of finesse. The power hitter will
either thank you for the reminder
or wrap your putter around your
neck. Be very careful if you spot
one on the hole behind you—no
matter how far away you think
you are from the last tee area.

Some Places
to Play

 THE
COUNTRY
CLUB

This is your little haven away
from it all—your little weekend
paradise. Here you can play a
round or two, go for a swim,
spend time with the whole family, have dinner, gossip, and
pose for a portrait entitled "The
Typical Suburban Weekend."
You'd better be able to hold your
own on the course (not to mention in business and in the bedroom) because no form of
communication has yet been in-

vented to surpass the speed at which news travels around The Country Club.

 THE HOTEL RESORT

Resort courses are great because you never have to see them again if you're having one of those days. The nicest part about these vacation courses is that you have the opportunity to meet, and lie to, perfect strangers about how well you usually do back home on more familiar territory. Another positive aspect to playing at a resort is that you can miss other fun-filled activities like shuffleboard, Simon Says (the adult version), and dance classes.

 THE GOLF RESORT

This is where you go to eat, drink, and sleep golf. It's the all-around, all-encompassing golf sabbatical—provided it doesn't rain. Bad weather means you'll have to do other things, and "other things" don't really exist at a "good" golf resort.

 THE GOLF COMMUNITY

Life by the fairway, a view of the green—what more could you want? Buying a condo on a golfing facility is the latest in total involvement and dedication to your game. You must, however, adapt to the lifestyle. You can no longer throw outdoor barbeques; must not argue loudly before sundown; must let anyone and everyone play through your porch or patio if necessary; and must never ever place a flagstick on your property or buy green drapes. If you don't mind your swimming pool doubling as a water hazard on the 14th, this is the ideal way to be close to the game.

THE PUBLIC PARK

Public courses run the gamut. Some are well maintained and quite challenging, whereas on others you'll lose a ball hit 100 yards straight down the "fairway." You may find yourself teamed up with anyone from a semipro to an escaped convict. The trick is to maintain your cool and poise even as you avoid hitting the dog catching a Frisbee on the 15th green and the topless sunbather in the sand trap on 17. Your worst enemy on many a public course will be the sprinkler system, which is often turned on in one spot for six to eight weeks, creating new water hazards.

The Stance

A convenient method of learning how to place the feet correctly is to check yourself on linoleum or other composition tiles, which are, unfortunately, difficult to find on most golf courses. It is a good idea to pull up a few squares from the kitchen floor and tuck them away in your golf bag for tee-off time in the morning.

Setting 4 to 6 square feet of tiles down on the teeing area, hold your feet together as though at attention, then spread them evenly apart until each comes to rest on a line, about shoulder-width apart. If you have extremely wide shoulders, you shouldn't wear very tight pants—or very short skirts. Your feet now run squarely along the lines, neither flared out nor pigeon-toed. Then, leaving the right as it is, turn the toes of the left approximately 20 degrees to the left, in the direction where you'd like the ball to go.

If you keep the weight evenly distributed on both feet, you will have the basic golf stance that strikingly resembles a common stance in men's room urinals.

Naturally, if you're a lefty, this doesn't apply to you. A lefty should either reverse the procedure or give up the game entirely.

There are modifications of this stance for putting, chipping, pitching, and relieving oneself behind a tree. Some other lesser-known stances include "the interlocking stance," which is the counterpart to the interlocking grip, except it involves wrapping one's legs around each other several times, and thus has been known to cause extreme discomfort during the follow-through. "The two seats of the bus stance," whereby your legs are spread wide enough to take up two spaces if you were seated, not to mention throwing your hips into another time zone when you try to swing. And, finally, there's the ever-popular "step-in stance," where you step into the pitch by moving the ol' front foot and hit a long foul ball, which in golf is a bit worse than a mere "strike one."

It's important to flare the left foot out as well as keep the right foot straight for several reasons. First, if you don't, someone will tell you to, and second, as the club is swung back you need support to balance the weight of the body as the momentum of the clubhead forces it to pivot to the right knee, through the twisting of the hips and the turning of the shoulders. If you follow this by putting your right foot forward, then pulling it back, twice consecutively, followed by turning the body in a complete 360-degree circle, you not only have a golfing stance but you're doing the Hokey-Pokey.

The momentum also requires the left knee to bend in so that it points behind the ball, not stuck out so that it points in front of the ball. If you have a trick knee, you may find yourself making trick shots whereby your knee is pointing wherever it wants to and your ball is going every which way but straight. Exaggerated bending of either or both knees, however, will have you either divoting badly or on your knees praying—or both.

It's a good idea to remember whenever and wherever you see two lines running a parallel, to practice your stance, unless the two lines are on the interstate.

The Swing of Things

How do you achieve the perfect golf swing? Simple answer, you don't. There is no "ideal swing" for everyone. You can, if you so choose, read the books, the magazine articles, and buy the videotapes by dozens of top pros, showing you how they've perfected their swing, but what you'll end up with is a combination Bobby Jones stance, Arnold Palmer backswing, Lee Trevino downward swing, Hale Irwin follow-through, and an Elmer Fudd shot. Why? Because somewhere in the making of this Herculean swing is you, the average golfer with decent skills. Somewhere in the course of interpreting what works so well for the in-shape, play every day, highly skilled pros, you'll invariably inject a flaw or two, or three . . .

Don't feel bad, just accept that no matter how much you study, your swing will still be the one that best suits you. There are factors that these books, tapes, and magazines can't take into account. For example, are you making the adequate compensation for that potbelly? Are

you naturally pigeon-toed? Are your arms long? Legs too short? Ladies, are you better endowed in the chest region than Nancy Lopez? These are factors that enter into your very own swing.

In developing your own personal swing, examine what comes from your own life experiences. For example, do you have a good low-ball swing in softball or baseball? Can you utilize your ability to cast a fishing rod? What stance do you use while vacuuming? What teacher made you stand in the corner keeping your head down? Use these aspects of your life when putting together your swing. Years of therapy might be helpful in getting to know "the real you" so you can find your very own unique swing.

Choosing Your Club

The familiar list of club choice and distance includes the driver at 240 yards and up, the 2 wood at 220 to around 250, the 3 wood in the 200 to 240 range, and so on, down through the irons and wedges. Your choice may, however, be different. And why not? After all, if the club always did what it was supposed to do, the game would be simple and your hair wouldn't be falling out.

Some golfers are convinced that they can't hit with a wood and will pull out the old 3 iron from 280 yards away, whereas others who don't do well with the irons select a wood for any shot over 90 yards. Then there are those who figure that the higher the shot, the better they're doing. These are the guys (and gals) popping 7-iron shots down the fairway. On the other hand, you have the golfer who's given up all hope of getting the ball in the air and simply wants distance on a grounder. Seventy-five yards from the green? They'll roll it on with a 2 iron.

Because you can only carry 14 clubs, according to the "official" rules of golf, you must choose beforehand which clubs to leave behind. The choice is simple. Leave behind the clubs you can't hit with, except of course the putter. So what if you have nothing in your bag between a 3 iron and a pitching wedge? If you can't use 'em, the hell with 'em.

If you're down to four or five clubs that you like, however, it will then look better to add some of the other clubs just for aesthetic purposes. You can arrange your bag as follows: clubs I can hit with on one side and clubs I hate on the other side. It's also nice to carry a full set to give others the impression that you are making some great calculated choice. No one has to know that you've chosen among the four clubs you really like. You might even remember to get a little dirt on some of those shiny "other" clubs that came with the set, just to appear proficient in their use.

For the average golfer it is proper, somewhat routine, and even expected, that after one or two mis-hits, immediately to check the number on the club, and shake your head indicating that your shot failed because you chose the wrong club. This won't work as a sufficient excuse more than twice in a given round, so use it wisely.

The proper method of club selection should take into consideration: distance, wind, lie, slope, and other stuff like that. However, other methods of club selection do exist for the average golfer—such as:

1. Use what someone else used.
2. Use the club you last hit a good shot with.
3. Use the club that you're holding so you don't have to walk back to your bag.
4. Use the only clean club left in your bag.
5. Pick randomly and hope for the best.
6. Eenie-meenie-miney-moe.

Don't let books, lists, and other people dictate what clubs you should use. Decide based on what you feel like using— what best suits your own game. After all, a fellow named Stanley Doyle was a bogey golfer with just a 5 iron. Talk about traveling light!

Putting

This seemingly simple task has baffled mankind since the invention of the game. The idea of having come so far with so much effort leads many a golfer to believe that he or she should automatically, by the will of God, be allowed to play this part of the game with relative ease. Since you've just traveled 450 yards in a mere three or four swings of the club, there is no way you should ever have to travel those last 30 feet in more than two! Unfortunately, as all golfers know, it's not quite that simple.

To excel at putting you first have to be able to read the green, which means that with the naked eye you can determine the exact geometric angle and distance between your ball and the cup, while including the texture and speed of the green, weight of your putter, and with how much force you should strike the ball. Once you've calculated this mathematical formula (X = distance + slope $\times$ texture, divided by power + acceleration $\times$ number of times you've blown such putts), you're almost there.

Now it's time to position yourself. There are many such workable putting positions, some with your feet close together, some more widespread, some holding the club with elbows pointed out, others holding the club farther down, and so on. Putting styles run the gamut from those who poke to those who stroke—there are flickers, sweepers, striders, those who putt stiff armed, those who crouch, those who slouch, and those whose contortions have not yet been defined. Nevertheless, the objective is the same. Get the ball close, "within three feet," they say, and then into the cup within a reasonable amount of time—like before your partners doze off or collapse from the heat.

Many golfers, in their quest for endless conversation topics, attempt to sink those 30 footers. These same golfers are often seen trying to then sink 12 footers that overran from their previous attempts at glory. These same golfers are often then seen hovering over a 3 footer, which, if missed, would mean holing out in four, a concept that closely rivals a stay of execution.

Other golfers, aware of the "3-foot" nucleus, attempt to sneak up on the cup. Using the principle that if they were to go a couple of feet beyond the hole they'd instantly be blown off the face of the earth, these golfers close that 30-foot gap to a closer, more manageable 12 feet, by taking it easy. They then narrow it down to a mere 3 feet, figuring that the ball, having not yet noticed the cup, will be tricked into falling in on the next

one. Should this not happen, they too face the dreaded 4 putt!

Thus, 3 putting is a sad but real part of life and 2 putting is an art form that's highly underappreciated. Sculpting has its place in museums, Renaissance artwork is revered, millions are paid for a Picasso, but what about the ability to place the ball in the cup in a mere TWO putts? Are those who've achieved this artistic mastery given their proper place among the giants of the art world?

Fifty million dollars for a Van Gogh? But could he 2 putt? Only if he could was the money well spent.

Dropping the Ball

A player is supposed to drop a ball when he or she is unable to play a stroke. The ball should be held at shoulder height and at arm's length and dropped. It is supposed to land as close as possible to the previous position but not closer to the hole. The rules have changed over the years. At one time the player's opponent dropped the ball, at another time it was the caddie, and at one point a professional "dropper" was a part of many pro tournaments.

Over the years, drop rules have included which way to face, which fingers to hold the ball between, and how many times to spin in a circle counting five Mississippi's. Other rules pertaining to dropping the ball include:

1. If no one is looking it is proper to drop the ball with a slight wrist action, flipping it 2 to 5 yards closer to the hole.
2. A player who drops the ball in casual water must pay for the cleaning and pressing of the pants of those who were splattered.
3. Should the ball be dropped on very firm ground and proceed to bounce up and strike the golfer in the head, he or she is entitled to take all the time necessary for medical attention and to wait until the rest of the foursome stops laughing.
4. A ball may not be dropped from a moving cart or onto a moving cart with a note that reads "Please deposit on green."

Golf Etiquette

Almost as important as knowing the rules is knowing how to "behave" on the course. Here are some courtesies to remember.

1. Repair and replace divots, glue branches back on trees, repair benches smashed by reckless prac-

tice swings or tantrums, and rake sand traps, but not while others are in them.
2. Never drive an electric cart into a sand trap, onto a green, too close to a water hazard, or over an opponent.
3. If, while you're searching for a ball, players behind you are striking up poker games or betting who can balance a ball on their 9 iron longer, then it's time to let them play through.
4. Try not to create new lavatories on the course, especially in the cup, sand traps, or water hazards.
5. Never realign sprinkler heads to face your opponents.
6. When a player is putting you should not stand directly behind the hole or with one foot covering the cup.
7. Never confuse the following foursome by sticking the flagstick into a part of the green other than the cup.
8. Never toss a golf club, bag, or caddie onto the putting green.
9. Try not to drive over an opponent's ball with your cart or wedge it into the ground with the heel of your shoe.
10. Keep the sound from the baseball game on your portable TV turned down.
11. Never stick the two plastic balls that mark the tee area under your shirt to impersonate Dolly Parton.
12. Never put out a cigar in the

cup or on your opponent's shoe.

13. Make at least some minimal effort to return all borrowed or rented clubs.

14. Don't leave beer cans on the fairway or greens; that's what bunkers are for.

15. Never offer unsolicited advice to someone bigger than yourself.

Guest Etiquette

If you find yourself invited to play at someone else's club, it can be rather intimidating. Often they have rules you're not familiar with, which usually become evident as you drive in through the exit at the parking lot and attempt to park in a "member's only" space.

Once you've ventured out of your car, all eyes will focus on you as you enter the clubhouse. It's advisable to be well dressed but not ostentatious. Seven gold chains may be overkill, and matching pants, shoes, and golf bag are unnecessary. Dress nicely, check your fly, and proceed. Lady golfers might double check their hair, because you'll be scrutinized twice as closely.

It's not advisable for golfers, especially female, to change clothes in the car. There should be locker-room facilities available. Make a concerted effort to behave in the locker room—after all, all glances are coming your way. Be courteous, shut off your video camera, don't give a club member a wedgie, and if there's a locker room attendant, don't toss him or her a pile of clothes and ask to have them ironed and returned with no starch.

Use common sense in the confines of an unfamiliar club. Roses and freshly-grown chrysanthemums shouldn't be used for practice shots. If there's food served, stuffing as much as possible into a zippered compartment of your bag (for later) is generally considered impolite, so be sure no one is looking. Should you be introduced to a longstanding member of the club, do not remark that he looks like he's been standing a little too long. And remember, onion dip is not for putting out cigar butts—that's what clam dip is for.

When on the course, it's advisable not to make too many assumptions. For all you know, the tennis courts may be in play, so don't just assume you can take a drop shot. Don't be afraid to ask questions. Ask where the bathroom is as you head into the bushes. Inquire whose window your slice just broke. Seek information on the exact value of the statue your practice swing just dented—was it a bust of the founder of the club or just a popular duffer?

When playing at a friend's or associate's club, it's a nice gesture to offer to pay for something—the drinks, the green fee, the caddies, ladies from an escort service, and such. Remember, the operative word is *offer* to pay. A good host won't let you.

Visiting unfamiliar clubs can be fun. Should you decide, however, that you *never* wish to return, and have no desire to continue your relationship with the host, here are some tips on how *not* to be invited back.

1. Wear your spikes into the dining room—and don't clean them.
2. Bring a date to the locker room.
3. Park your electric cart on the practice putting green—and take the keys.
4. Save your divots, and add them to the salad bar.
5. Play the absolute best or worst round of your life. You'll either embarrass the host or show him up. Works every time.

Par-3 Pressure

Why is it that if your opponent has the audacity to tee off into a fierce wind on a 175 yard par 3 with a 9 iron, you suddenly think you should be macho enough to do the same?

Among the most amazing phenomenons in golf is that of par-3 "peer" pressure. This is that gut feeling that whatever club those preceding you have used, it is the club that you'll use too—despite the fact the others are not on the green. So what if you know deep down in your heart that you really want to use a 5 iron when they've all teed off with 7 irons? You can't appear to be a golf wimp! Thus you tee off with the club that everyone else used, and, like the others, blame the tee, the wind, the grip, and picking your head up for your failing shot.

Par-3 Pressure, known as PTP, is widespread in the amateur and Sunday golfer ranks. Most common among male golfers, it's added as many as seven strokes to an otherwise good round. Golf therapists believe that the problem evolves from an inferiority complex stemming from playing pitch and putt and miniature golf courses during childhood. When everyone else scribbled something obscene on the windmill hole at the local miniature golf course, did you feel a need to do the same? When the kids on the pitch and putt course kicked their opponent's putt away, did you retaliate? These are early signs of PTP to watch for.

Often players will try to cover up PTP by quickly returning their club to the bag in order to hide the fact that they used an 8 while everyone else used a 9 iron. Although this should help a player's game, it doesn't, because the player is concentrating harder on concealing his clubface from his peer group than on his shot. Other players simply lie about the club they used, risking extreme embarrassment if they're caught before they can hustle it back into the bag. For so many golfers, however, on the tee, it's "Do as the others do." It's sad to watch a PTP golfer's 9-iron shot fall short of the green when you know that deep down they wish they'd had the inner fortitude to use a 7.

Par-3 Pressure is hard to conquer, but it can be easier if the golfer is willing to admit that he's not a power hitter. Take pride in your short game, work on being the best putter you can be, and perhaps one day those of you with PTP will be able to step up to that Par-3 tee area and proudly announce, "I'm using a 6 iron!"

Once one PTP golfer steps forward, others will do the same. It does, however, help tremendously if you then land it on the green.

The Mental Side of Golf

A great part of golf, like any other sport, is "mental." If you think you can play well, maybe you will. Doubtful, but possible. The average golf enthusiast should immediately forget about little things like "par for the course." Par exists only for you to have something to dream or fantasize about on a quiet day at the office or when your spouse has dozed off early.

Par for a particular hole, however, is another story. Some golfers ask for just one or two per round and they feel their mission is complete. An occasional par is good mentally if you accept the fact that it might not happen again for the next 3, 4, or 16 holes. Savor it as you bend to retrieve the ball from the cup. Replay the par 4 in your mind. When you find yourself uttering those classic words, "Now if I could just do that on every hole," realize the humor in the statement—smile—laugh. If you take those words seriously, you're in deep s---!

Appreciate the bogey for what it is. It's damn close to par, perhaps just one screwup away. Feel good, tell yourself "Nobody's perfect," and always remind yourself that in England a bogey is considered par for the average golfer.

Don't frown on double bogeys. They are, for many an average golfer, quite commonplace. Keep yourself mentally in check. Remind yourself of the tough week you've had, the problems at work, how hard it is to make ends meet, the agony of trying to pay off a mortgage, not to mention braces for the kids and a fuel pump for the car. With all that on your mind, you're pretty damn lucky to walk away with just a double bogey!

Even though it glares at you from the scorecard, tell yourself you'll stop thinking about your miserable last hole from the moment you step up to the next tee. All right, from the moment you hit your next drive . . . okay, okay . . . you'll definitely stop thinking about it by the time you walk, or ride, to your second shot!

One way to stay mentally on track is to be an eternal optimist. So you hooked your drive onto the neighboring fairway—at least it had distance. So the divot went 30 yards beyond the shot, it could be a new divot-flying record. So the putt kept rolling another 9 feet beyond the cup, they'll be more impressed when you sink the 9-footer than an easy 2-footer anyway!

Another way to keep mentally sharp is to keep telling yourself, "Okay, this is the first shot of the rest of my game." Starting "now" you'll concentrate, play well, do all those things the instructors have been telling you. Strive for two good shots in a row, three . . . maybe four—okay, don't overdo it!

It's also a good idea to try thinking positively. Tell yourself, "I can drive it 225 yards straight down the fairway." "I know I can hit the green." "I'm positive I can clear that bunker." "I'm positive I'll hit the tree and lose the ball." "There's no way in hell I'll clear the water." Be certain! Be sure! Be positive about your game!

And finally, remember there's always a chance to improve. If you maintain the mental attitude that your game is "improving," you'll feel good out there on the course, even if it is a lie.

The Slice

Chronic slicers have a tendency to turn their hips and shoulders toward the target, thereby throwing the clubhead outside the line of flight. In other words, you're hitting the ball with left to right spin, or screwing up. In avoiding a slice you should feel no sense of reaching for the ball. The radius of your swing should be determined by a straight but not rigid left arm, and your knees should be bent just enough to let the clubhead touch the ground. There, now that we've solved that problem, here's what some of the great intellects of history had to say on the subject of slicing:

According to Freud: "The slice by a male golfer is his way of staying far back and reaching out for sex, attempting to extend his 'club' beyond its boundaries. While trying to strike with a forward thrust there is a hesitancy to follow through and a need to look at the results of your sexual actions before you've finished."

According to Einstein: "The slice is merely a physiological inadequacy of the projectory of the club and the ball to meet at a proper angle in time and motion."

According to Dr. Joyce Brothers: "Women slice because they feel unfulfilled sexually. They feel that they shouldn't commit themselves fully to their drive."

According to William Shakespeare: "The slice is a far, far more noble test of fortitude than thou thrusts upon one's inner being by merely so much as willingly punishing thineself on the putting green."

According to Confucius: "Slice is like man who talk straight but lean to the right."

According to Yogi Berra: "Any golf ball hasn't landed until it's landed."

According to Neil Armstrong: "Overcoming a slice is one small step for mankind, one giant leap for a Sunday golfer."

According to Ben Franklin: "Not now, I've got a kite to fly."

Gimme That Thing!

According to the rules of the game, artificial devices are not permitted. There are exceptions, however. Here is a list of what is and is not allowed on the course according to the rules.

1. Weighted head covers—Allowed
2. Regulation eyeglasses—Allowed and often encouraged by the foursome ahead of you.
3. A telescope—Unfortunately not allowed, but helpful if guiding your shots by star patterns.
4. A harmonica—Only allowed when waiting to tee off in the Deep South or playing a foursome on a prison golf release program.
5. A ball warmer—Not allowed, so keep it hidden deep in your bag.
6. A condom—If you find a good reason to use it, it's allowed.
7. A hand warmer—A hand warmer is allowed, especially if it's a member of the opposite sex.
8. An electronic ball finder—You'll probably need an electric ball finder finder just to find one.
9. A rifle—Allowed if the duffer ahead of you won't let you play through.
10. A fishing rod—Allowed at Pebble Beach.
11. A stethoscope—Allowed on Wednesdays only, by doctors who insist on "more thoroughly" examining a cut ball or the break in the green.
12. The Goodyear blimp—If you can afford it, you can use it to provide an overhead view of the course and cast an-

Two Types of Strategy

On the golf course, there are primarily two mind-sets when it comes to strategy. There's the aggressive golfer who believes in getting 225 yards from a 5 iron, and the conservative golfer who believes if the ball is in deep rough, get back to the fairway and don't attempt an amazing 160-yard shot through three trees and onto the green.

Basically here are the extremes of two different strategies. Hopefully, you'll settle somewhere in the middle.

THE "ULTRA"- CONSERVATIVE APPROACH	THE "VERY" AGGRESSIVE APPROACH
When facing a major water hazard, try to place the ball as close as possible. Then, rather than an easy chip over the hazard, take three extra shots going around it.	Ain't no mountain high enough. Ain't no river wide enough. The fun of the game is being able to clear any hazard from anywhere.
A 30-foot putt? No way! Make a 10-foot radius around the hole and get it in there. Then do the same with a 3-foot radius, then a 1-foot radius. So you 4 putt, at least you didn't overshoot the cup.	It's going in! Go for it with a bold putt seeking that dramatic "imagined" crowd roar as it goes in. So what if you run it 12 feet past the cup! Never pass up a chance for immortality.
In the sand? Just take that sand wedge and get it out, even if it only lands 3 yards away. The goal isn't to get a good well-planned shot here . . . possibly on the green, it's just to be out of that damn trap at any cost!	Sand, what sand? Ignore the fact completely and hit as though nothing is wrong. After all, a little sand isn't going to get in the way of a brilliant shot. Tee it up if no one's looking! Use a wood! Go for it!

noying shadows on opponents as they take their shots.

Golf Tip I

Don't let the right side dominate your downswing; it'll usually lead to a poor downswing path and a bad shot. Work up the strength in your left side by developing it. Take . practice swings with just your left arm alone. To make this feel less awkward, hold a book in your right arm—preferably a book about golf, or, if you reside in a large city, you might try the telephone directory. To avoid the temptation of using your right arm you might try placing your right hand under an open window and slamming it down, using just your left hand. This will both strengthen your left arm while totally eliminating any desire to use your right. Pretty soon you'll notice the improvement in downswing as your left side has been included—you'll also notice the swelling in your right hand. Nobody said golf was easy!

Golf Tip II

Imagine two ways to play a pitch, high or low. Then, imagine a third alternative, and that's way off course entirely. Decide which way is easier, considering the break, slope, speed of the surface, and how thick the neighboring woods are. Visualize your ball going on either the high route, the low route, or into the trees never to be seen again.

Once you're over the ball, concentrate only on making solid contact and impressing your client, boss, or partner. Keep in mind that those with you judge your business success on how well you play this shot, and that your impending financial future and that of your family ride on this, and only this pitch. Then relax and take your stroke. Nobody said golf didn't have its share of pressure.

Practice

PUTTING AROUND THE OFFICE

Putting in the office takes concentration, a secretary who won't barge in on you, and something to putt into. A wastepaper basket on its side has been replaced with automatic putting devices, which in many cases will return the ball to you, provided you don't miss the device entirely.

Substitutes for the putting machine include paper cups, pencil holders, your coffee mug, your son's or daughter's baby shoes, an A-cup bra, or a small potted plant holder (remove plant first).

Indoor putting requires reading the carpet properly. Usually shags and deep pile will result in a slower green. Often, that subtle mark in the green that helps you line up your putt can be reproduced by a coffee stain or two.

An indoor fan can help you recreate the breeze off the ocean on the 17th hole, whereas a few indoor potted trees add a woodsy feel to your office links. Green carpeting is also preferred.

It's a good idea to practice with some distractions for when you're putting close to the road, or when your partner's hayfever causes an impromptu sneezing attack. A good office distraction can be caused by leaving the volume on your answering machine turned up or leaving the

intercom on to hear typing and idle gossip.

To really sharpen your putting skills you might try putting in front of your boss's office door. Your aim is to get the ball as close to the door as possible without hitting it.

Another good way to improve how you read the green is to ask to putt in clients' and associates' offices where you're not familiar with the carpet. Often the conference room can provide a longer putting area plus distractions if a meeting is taking place.

For reading the slope of a green it's helpful to get an area rug large enough to establish some sort of break as the ball moves toward the so-called cup. To do so you can slide objects under portions of the rug, such as a book, old shoes, a computer keyboard, the company ledger, a secretary, and so on. This will allow you to read the break in the green more accurately.

For those who don't have the luxury of their own office, a doctor's waiting room is a nice quiet place to practice while imagining that the fish tank is a water hazard. On rainy days, visiting your in-laws can be tolerable as well as beneficial provided they have a carpeted area for you to use. Relatives are far more receptive to your putting in their homes if you pretend you're on the last hole of the (fill in their names) Open.

Apartment corridors, carpet and furniture stores, movie theater lobbies, and airplane aisles also provide the appropriate variety of carpeting for practice.

Because putting is such an integral part of the game, there's no reason not to practice at every opportunity—including hospital waiting rooms, outside your child's principal's office, inside your child's principal's office, on the red carpet awaiting a dignitary or head of state, or at a catering hall between the soup and main course at your cousin's wedding.

Every Place Is a Practice Area

With clubs in the trunk and balls in the glove compartment, the true golfer is ready to practice at any time. After all, how difficult can it be to lure a half-dozen youngsters out of a playground sandbox so that you can try out your new sand wedge?

To love the game is to find any excuse to practice it when you can't get to play. For example, a tour of movie stars' homes in Beverly Hills wouldn't be complete without taking full advantage of their manicured front lawns. If your son or daughter plays Little League baseball under the lights, you should get involved. Help out during batting and fielding practice. Once the game begins you'll have nine innings and two dozen bases on balls to do your thing out in deep right field where no one hits the ball anyway.

There are so many places one can practice. Public fountains provide a great opportunity to hit out of a lateral water hazard. And what golfer doesn't bring a pitching wedge on a picnic to see how close you can get your shot to the blanket?

There are so many places that are well designed for golf. For example: Do you know that with a 3 wood you can clear Niagara Falls? (Talk about a water hazard!) And how about that great fairway between the Washington Monument and the Lincoln Memorial? Ever stop to think why they created Central Park? And what do you think the infield at the racetrack is for?

5th HOLE—

Nobody Said It Was Easy

I'd like to make a living playing golf, but it wouldn't pay
the bills.

—*Mark Rypien,*
NFL quarterback

10 Popular Excuses You Tend to Hear Around Any Course

1. I picked my head up too soon.
2. I picked my head up too late.
3. It's too early in the morning; I'm not awake yet.
4. The ball is no good.
5. This grip is no good.
6. This course is no good.
7. Those damn grounds keepers!
8. The tee must have already been broken.
9. I ate too much for breakfast.
10. My shorts are riding up on me.

You Know You're Having a Bad Day When . . .

You run over your own foot with your electric cart.

Other golfers have nicknamed you "Shank."

You spend the majority of your day ripping the cellophane off new balls.

Your shoes are filled with enough sand to open your own private beach club.

You've lifted your head so often you have a crick in your neck.

The rest of your foursome huddles behind a bench as you tee off.

Your tee-off time for tomorrow has been revoked.

Your club membership has been revoked.

Your woods are too embarrassed to come out of the bag.

The course pro introduces you to a tennis instructor.

The course superintendent threatens you with legal action.

Birds flying south readjust their flight pattern to let you hit.

People are offering you good prices for your clubs.

Between the 9th and 10th holes, life insurance salesmen approach you in the clubhouse.

Golfing with the Boss

How to play the boss's way.

1. Compliment his or her backswing every third hole, even if there's an obvious flaw in it.
2. Never acknowledge their mishits, especially on the scorecard. If they forgot shanking

that 14-foot roller, it must have been your imagination.

3. Agree with your boss that there's something wrong with his or her clubs and never use one to prove otherwise.

4. If they ask you what they're doing wrong, pick something minor that they can easily correct. Ignore the obvious need for 200 lessons.

5. If he or she must drive the cart, don't argue. Pray, but don't look scared, even if your clubs and bag have just jumped ship.

6. Always offer to help your boss in the futile search for the ball that just cascaded into the Pacific Ocean.

7. Always lose, but keep it close.

8. Remember to mention how much fun you had.

9. Back up his or her stories the next day in the office, even if it means biting a pencil or two in half. "Yeah, that was a great shot you hit on 16," you'll respond, knowing deep down in your heart about the three preceding grounders.

A Bad Day on the Course

From a golfer's personal diary:

Missed tee-off time by 3 minutes thanks to traffic. Used waiting time to hit men's room after breakfast of runny eggs, burned toast, and bad coffee.

1st Hole—437 yards Par 4: Wind blows ball off tee. Split pants bending over to pick it up. Slice tee shot into nearby swimming pool. Holed out in 7.

2nd Hole—469 yards Par 4: After good drive, buried second shot so deep in sand trap that I seriously considered bringing in archaelogists to dig. Took third, fourth, and fifth shots to get out of sand trap. Got splinter from rake. Holed out in 7.

3rd Hole—237 Yards Par 3: Ball lands on edge of lateral water hazard. Hit good recovery shot, fall into lateral water hazard. Let elderly foursome play through while drying off. Holed out in 5.

4th Hole—421 Yards Par 4: Put third shot on green—wrong green. Japanese businessmen on 7th are not pleased. Holed out in 6. Electric cart drops dead on route to 5th tee. Attempt to use emergency phone—out of order. Wait for repairs, let foursome of nuns play through.

5th Hole—538 Yards Par 5: Par the hole! Left jacket back at tee area. Expend a lot of energy running back to get it.

6th Hole—159 Yards Par 3: Put tee shot right on green! Four putt! Holed out in 5.

When Can One Experience Course Interruptus?

There are very few acceptable reasons for a golfer to discontinue play. Once on the course, you're there for the duration. Here is a list of acceptable and unacceptable reasons to halt play:

UNACCEPTABLE	ACCEPTABLE
There is a danger of lightning.	Your score is beginning to look like your area code.
Your partner has been struck by lightning.	The Super Bowl is on. (Unacceptable if Denver's in it.)
You have been struck by lightning.	(Men) You encounter a sexy sunbather.
A sniper's running loose.	(Ladies) The club pro offers you private lessons.
The course has been closed down.	You've run out of snack food.
The course is being turned into a shopping center as you play.	
The club or committee has voted you out.	
Your spouse has filed divorce papers.	
Your spouse has run off with the course superintendent.	

7th Hole—431 Yards Par 4: Slice ball into thick wooded area. Look for ball, discover ball, discover beehive. Holed out in 6.

8th Hole—521 Yards Par 5: Rain. Discovered that last week's borrower of my umbrella forgot to return it. Holed out in a soggy 9.

9th Hole—134 Yards Par 3: Overclubbed tee shot lands on green—green station wagon in parking lot. Holed out in 5.

Go to snack bar. Get potato chips—stale. Partners try to trade me to another foursome—no takers.

10th Hole—431 Yards Par 4: Put third shot on cart path, causing minor four-cart fender bender. Quickly hit off cart path and into nearby ravine. Retrieve ball from ravine, accidentally drop 9 iron, never to be seen again. Hole out in 8! Lead partners to wrong tee-off area. Discover error after teeing off on 17th.

11th Hole—210 Yards Par 3: Hit 3-foot putt for par. Throw my back out taking ball from cup.

12th Hole—559 Yards Par 5: Rain begins again, with lightning. You guessed it. Fortunately nothing serious. Take brief rest as foursome of 13-year-old juvenile delinquents plays through. Holed out in 8.

13th Hole—406 Yards Par 4: The way it's been going I'd just as soon skip lucky number 13. Nevertheless, shoot a birdie! No problems—there must be something wrong.

14th Hole—465 Yards Par 4: Fail to hear golfer on 15th yell Fore! Nothing serious, just grazed. Place third shot inches from fallen branch. Go to move it only to discover fallen branch is actually hissing snake . . . Holed out in 7.

15th Hole—428 Yards Par 4: Strike up conversation with attractive young woman in following foursome now waiting as we tee off. Impress her with 65-yard pathetic rolling drive. Holed out in 7.

16th Hole—210 Yards Par 3: Drive ball onto green near fence where local kids are watching. Local kids steal ball. Par anyway!

17th Hole—545 Yards Par 5: Drive sends ball 265 yards straight ahead and clubhead 232 yards right behind it. Slice second shot into grounds keeper's equipment shed. Play through. Unknowingly give member of foursome coin valued at $3,000 to mark ball with (found out a week later). Holed out in 7.

18th Hole—190 Yards Par 3: Need 5-foot putt for birdie. Torrential downpour; play abruptly halted.

Return to clubhouse and drink

two beers. Find out men's room is closed. Flirt with attractive young waitress—grounds keeper's niece. He's not pleased (nor thrilled that I played through his equipment shed). Brave member of four-some offers me lift home. I accept. Slight fender bender; he should be out of hospital in a week. Note on refrigerator door . . . wife left me for a PGA pro. Horrible day—shot a 102!

6th HOLE—

Places to Swing

It's almost impossible to remember how tragic a place the world is when one is playing golf.

—*Robert Lynd,*
sociologist

A Few
Noteworthy Holes

THE 7th HOLE
(PEBBLE BEACH, CAL)

This 110-yard par-3 hole sits right on the edge of the Pebble Beach course's favorite water hazard—the Pacific Ocean. Other hazards on this little hole include deep sand traps surrounding 75 percent of the green and numerous shutterbugs taking pictures, because this is considered the most photographed hole in the world. Regulations governing moving a ball resting against a tripod and how to chip over a used film canister are part of this photogenic hole. Besides being a par 3, the hole has its own F-stop reading and a guide to the best possible shots—with the camera, that is.

THE 18th HOLE
(PEBBLE BEACH)

This 540-yard par-5 hole gives you the best view of the Pacific Ocean you're likely to see from any course on the West Coast. In fact, your mission is basically to clear a large part of it on your drive, unless you care to skillfully work your way around it. Essentially, knowing at all times, as you prepare to hit each and every shot—even putts—that the ocean is oh so near, and oh

such a "hazard of hazards," will entice you to hit one shot into it, even it you've already holed out. It's like trying to eat one potato chip—you can't do it—and you can't leave the hole feeling satisfied unless you make just one splash.

THE 13th HOLE
(AUGUSTA NATIONAL)

This 485-yard par-5 hole gives you two options. You can either follow the fairway over streams and around the bend or you can aim to the right, clear a few paltry trees and some water, and cut 150 yards off the journey while adding a few gray hairs along the way. But what is golf if you don't live dangerously?

Opting for the more daring route and getting to the green quickly is to your advantage because you might spend an inordinate amount of time on the green, which, like so many at Augusta, is huge. In fact, players with cellular phones have discovered that the green covers two area codes. A mere 50-foot putt is nothing on this spacious landing area. The usually "fast" green has been used for softball games on a quiet day. Be prepared to put muscle into your putts, and never volunteer to hold the flagstick—the walk from the pin to your ball and back may exhaust you for the rest of the day.

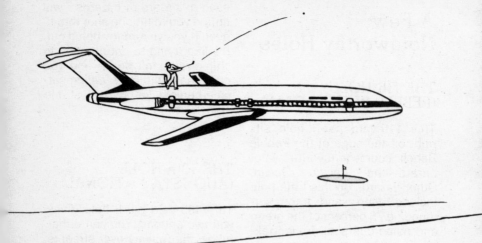

THE 6th HOLE (KOOLAN ISLAND, AUSTRALIA)

The 860-yard par-7 sixth at Koolan Island Golf Course in Australia is not only the longest hole in all of golf, but includes one of the most unique hazards of any course in the world—airplanes. The hole is on land that is also used as part of the local airstrip, and therefore you must let all incoming or outgoing flights play, or fly through. Striking a plane is a penalty, and finding the ball afterward is a miracle. Playing this endless hole requires great strength, radar equipment, and a working golf cart to get you to the other end. It's also nice to know there are outhouses along the way. At 860 yards there should be a restaurant as well!

THE 16th HOLE (CYPRESS POINT, MONTEREY, CAL)

This simple 200-yard par-3 hole is designed for the amusement of the porpoise, as they watch countless golf balls, clubs, and an occasional golfer land in the Pacific Ocean. The objective here, other than amusing the sea mammals, is to get the ball onto a green situated high upon the rocks on a tiny island that even Gilligan and the Skipper would have trouble finding. Bing Crosby once aced the hole, then again he had his own tournament. If you do the same, you might get your own tourney as well. Meanwhile, bring scuba gear and a box of XXX balls for this one.

THE 12th HOLE (HAMPTON CLUB, ST. SIMONS ISLAND, GA)

This is for anyone who really enjoyed the game of leapfrog. With a few sturdy elevated cart bridges, this hole allows you the fun and challenge of trying to place your ball on not one but several little islands on your way to the green. Fear not, the alligator-infested marshlands become more appealing after plummeting several shots into the water. Another comforting note about this particular hole is that it is followed by three more just like it. But for our own purposes we'll select just this one and hope that you appreciate what course designer Joe Lee had to say about this bevy of holes. "Every golfer wants a challenge, but he doesn't want to be out there fighting the Korean War." If the quote doesn't make a lot of sense, remember it's from a guy who designs courses around alligators.

THE 10th HOLE (BARTON CREEK, TX)

This is a must for those with vertigo or ski-jumping fantasies. The 110-foot drop from the tee area to the fairway discourages golfers from leaving anything behind at the tee area. The course director has explained that on this hole a shot is measured not by distance, but by hang time. It's strongly advised that you test your brakes well in advance when parking near the 10th hole.

Courses of the 90s

Here are a few of the "new" courses you might not yet be familiar with.

THE THOUSAND ISLAND GOLF RESORT—A great, challenging course awaits you if you love water hazards and bridges. Speedboats are advised over electric carts, and bring six- to eight-dozen range balls.

THE DEATH VALLEY GOLF AND TENNIS RESORT—In 120-degree heat no one dares play tennis. Golf is a bit grueling unless you enjoy a little fairway with your 200-yard sand traps. Snakes are counted as loose implements, and there aren't many water hazards, but when you find one, go for it! If you can air-condition your bag, do it—then climb in.

THE NEW LAS VEGAS GOLF RESORT AND DINNER THEATER—It's golf the Las Vegas way. Take a stroke, pull a handle. Let the showgirls wash your balls as you enjoy a few rounds of poker while waiting to tee off. Every hole has the distance posted, along with the betting line.

THE BERMUDA TRIANGLE GOLFING SOCIETY—Your ball is not all you're likely to lose.

THE SAN ANDREAS FAULT LINE GOLFING SOCIETY—Who said golfers aren't daring? This is the only course where the grounds keepers don't have to move the holes—they move themselves. Never give up on a putt that falls an inch short, it might suddenly roll right in—or onto the next fairway.

THE NIAGARA FALLS GOLF CLUB—The new course is nothing spectacular but the water hazard on 14 is one hell of a challenge.

THE "NEW" ICELAND GOLFING CLUB—The old Iceland golfing club is still thawing out, so the new one has been built for the true lover of "Winter Rules." The word *Mush* will get your dog-driven cart moving, but as for your arms and legs, you're on your own. Putt quickly before the break in the green melts.

GREAT ADVENTURE'S LION SAFARI GOLF RESORT—The new combination lion country safari–golf course has speeded up play considerably. Pack a tranquilizer gun in your bag, and when shooting, remember that you may not have the luxury of a practice shot.

THE GOLF CLUB AT DOLLYWOOD—Dolly Parton's amusement park now has a fun, but mountainous course with larger-than-usual cups.

THE NEW CENTRAL PARK GOLF FACILITY—New York's largest park now has a 9-hole course. Each hole is named after a city subway line, which may explain the turnstiles at each tee area. When on the course, it's a good idea to try and get to your ball before someone else does.

Course Descriptions

Usually the description of a course is right on the money. In fact, many courses are not done justice in print—the layout and majestic beauty of the course can only be captured in person. There are, however, those few courses that sound better than they are. Here are a few advertisements for courses and what they (hopefully don't) really mean.

WHAT THE AD SAYS	WHAT THE AD MIGHT REALLY MEAN
VERMONT: Scenic mountainous course with many elevation changes	We tried in vain to put a summer course on our winter ski slopes.
Challenging 18-hole lakeside par-3 course. Seven of last nine holes have water on them	We didn't have room for a bigger course, so we crammed one in around the lake. Bring plenty of range balls and watch out for fishermen.
Beautifully built into 1,800 acres of hardwood forest. Thick foliage surrounds large undulating greens.	We could only afford to have 800 acres of trees cut down. You can bounce your shot off 16 varieties of oak, then have the thrill of 3 putting.

WHAT THE AD SAYS	**WHAT THE AD MIGHT REALLY MEAN**
Many holes border on the ocean, whereas others are flanked by our luxurious vacation resort facilities.	You can either hook your shot into the ocean or slice one into the pool. Relax and concentrate on your game between beach bums, bathing beauties, lifeguard whistles, and the shuffleboard set.
Varied terrain and skillfully laid-out course will test every club in your bag. Level fairways give way to rolling hills and water comes into play on seven holes.	Architects had major feud over layout and divided up course. Perhaps a bit too much variety— you may even find a windmill hole!
Championship course, in midst of renovation program, still quite challenging.	Do you consider clearing a bulldozer with a 5 iron a challenge?
Spectacular views from most holes. Course features natural stream, two ponds, and a brook. Eleven varieties of wildflowers can be found growing along the back nine.	Bring a camera, take a nature walk, drink natural spring water, and enjoy the scenery. The course? We only built it for aesthetic reasons.

Just Another Typical Course

Here's a look at our very own "unofficial" golf course.

HOLE #1 465 Yards Par 4 "THE LONG AND NARROW"

The first hole proceeds down a long, very narrow fairway. Don't go for distance, go for accuracy, because the fairway is only 3 feet across at its widest. The grass in the surrounding deep rough has never been touched or altered in 30 years, so it is quite thick, adding to your desire to stay on the fairway. The only bunker is right in front of the green. It's not large but deep, and you should take the escalator back after using a wedge to hit your shot up—and we mean up, and out of there.

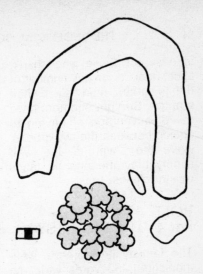

HOLE #2 207 Yards Par 3 "OFF THE WALL, OR FENCE"

Feel free to use the driver if you wish. The green sits right in front of the rear fence to the driving range. Thus you can bounce any drive off the fence and you'll have a good chance of landing on the green. The green, however, can be very fast, because it's been Scotchgarded.

HOLE #3 475 Yards Par 4 "TEMPTATION"

It's about 250 yards straight out, and a dogleg right. There's an oak tree and a Mobile station at the dogleg, so you won't miss it. The last 60 yards are uphill, so you can't see the green until you get there. This is to secure the surprise once you land on it. Let's just say it's challenging for married men.

HOLE #4 449 Yards Par 4 "THE SNAKE PIT"

This hole has no fairway. The first 220 yards are paved, so expect extra distance on your roll, or bounce, in this case. The green is surrounded by four large bunkers, one of which is stocked with poisonous snakes. Use a 9 iron to club the snakes, then hit with your wedge.

HOLE #5 599 Yards Par 3 "THE IQ TEST"

Yes, it's a par 3 because the long horseshoe-shaped fairway wraps around a dozen oak trees, but the green actually sits some 120 yards to the left of the tree. Use a 9 iron to plunk it over the trees, or take the long route with your driver, and so on. Your choice of long or short road to the green will help determine your golfer's IQ.

HOLE #6 478 Yards 462 Yards Par 4/4 "TWO FOR ONE"

The fairway is wide and lined by beautiful trees. A majestic breeze sweeps over this hole from the south, bringing an aroma of Chow Fu's Chinese Take Out. Ahead you'll see two—yes, two—greens separated by a small pond. The hole is easy for those who shank, slice, hook, or do any number of things other than hit a ball straight. Straight shooters have the disadvantage of having to decide between the two greens, while the "Average Joe" will simply play the one he lands on—or closest to.

HOLE #7 434 Yards
Par 4 "THE BIG EASY"

The fairway is a breeze, well-manicured, 50 yards wide, no bunkers . . . no problems. The green, however, is on an 82-degree angle, and the worn grass has been replaced by linoleum, which makes reading the green a nightmare.

HOLE #8 153 Yards
Par 3 "STRAIGHT UP"

The "telephone pole" is what they've nicknamed this one. Tee it up high, because all 153 yards are straight up. Once you pop it onto the green, don't let it roll back off!

HOLE #9 448 Yards
Par 4 "BACK HOME"

This one brings you back to the clubhouse—literally. The green is located in the 19th hole tavern. It's an easy iron shot with the tavern windows open. If they're closed, you may use a wood for extra power. The green poses few problems, unless you roll under the jukebox.

HOLE #10 245 Yards
Par 3 "THE SPACE SAVER"

Due to a limited amount of space for the course, this one utilizes the clubhouse with a roof tee area and has the green located in the parking lot. Don't park anywhere near it. The only hazards here are bad drivers and falling off the roof.

HOLE #11 456 Yards
Par 4 "THE DESSERT"

All 456 yards are sand trap, making it a Middle Easterner's dream hole. Two small bunkers filled with grass are located 50 yards in front of the green. Polish off your sand wedge and when you get to the green, also known as "the oasis," empty out your shoes.

HOLE #12 16 Yards
Par 2 "THE LITTLE EASY"

All right, so it's a miniature golf hole. This little doozy, and we mean little, can throw off even the best. Suddenly your day of heavy hitting has been reduced to getting through the windmill and the loop-d-loop. Many a scratch golfer has joked his or her way to a 4 on this one.

HOLE #13 723 Yards
Par 7 "PACK A LUNCH"

This endless wonder tests your stamina. Mostly uphill and without fairway, you may need to utilize one of the two rest areas along the way, both equipped with food, lodging, and restroom facilities. The trees along the route are quite lovely, and the hole overlooks a breathtaking, picturesque landscape. There are photo spots marked along your journey, tour guides available, and even a Fotomat.

HOLE #14 431 Yards Par 4 "THE BUDGET HOLE"

No tee area, no fairway, no benches, traps with no sand, no green and a cup with no flagstick, this is the unkempt lowbudget hole. Don't even bother trying the water fountain.

HOLE #15 389 Yards Par 4 "THE OFF RAMP"

Other than a dogleg left and a bunker filled with whipped cream, this is a fairly ordinary fairway. The green, however, is located in the center of a circular off ramp from Interstate 92. A good test of your short game, this one will have you dodging traffic if you over or under hit.

HOLE #16 500 Yards Par 5 "THE SHOPPER'S HOLE"

Hit your approach shot to the right and you should land smack in the middle of the pro shop, which is actually your best bet. The left will send you down a ravine into the tar pits. A 9 iron from aisle two should get you from the pro shop to the green and, with a purchase, the course pro will even instruct you on hitting out of the shoe department.

HOLE #17 154 Yards Par 3 "OLD SOGGY"

For no apparent reason, this is that one hole where the sprinkler system is always on. No matter where you hit, you need your umbrella at all times on this one. It's also advisable to buy Totes—with cleats, of course—because the ground is well beyond soggy. The sprinklers are body-temperature activated so that whenever someone is within a 400-yard radius they'll go on, and stay on. The green is naturally very slow, and players often mark their shots with an available water buoy.

HOLE #18 512 Yards Par 5 "ENDLESS HOLE"

Do not slice on this one! There's a skunk farm to the right. The fairway is all downhill, meaning with a tail wind and a nice roll, you can easily turn a 200-yard drive into a 350-yard beauty. The problem is the green—there's no cup. Arguments over exactly where to place it have caused the matter to be taken to court. An injunction has prevented the two architects (from opposing golfing factions) to alter the green until a settlement is reached. A par 5 is generally achieved after landing on the green in two or three, and then putting a couple of shots around aimlessly until you've had enough for the day.

All in all, this Par 70 *Unofficial Golfer's Handbook* Course provides a tidy little challenge to even the boldest golfers. You may come back with more items then you started with, including a pet snake, but it'll be worth it for the photos on 13 if nothing else.

The Driving Range

In Japan, due to an overwhelming love for the game and a limited amount of space, there are now three-tier driving ranges where one can translate phrases like "Wow, the guy upstairs just hit a great shot."

Throughout the United States, a trip to the driving range can provide some encouragement for those rounds on the links. Of course, if the person next to you stands 5 foot one and is hitting 3-iron shots over the far back fence, it's going to put a damper on your fun. Nevertheless, the driving range gives right-handed golfers a chance to practice their game and left-handed golfers a chance to look for that rare lefty tee that hasn't been squashed or conveniently moved out of the way by the right-handers.

The "true" golfer practices with various clubs off the tee and off the synthetic "grass." The rest of the gallery tees off trying strictly for distance or hoping to hit a line drive off the little truck picking up the balls.

The driving range provides an opportunity to get into a rhythm, as you hit one 200 yarder after another—straight—beautiful. It's almost like playing tennis! Essentially it's just like golf, without the walking, changing clubs, hazards, scoring, or putting.

Even on the driving range there are moments to forget—like when you accidentally pop the plastic tee off the mat and 20 yards forward—or that one shot that makes a resounding ricocheting sound as it careens off the partition, or that moment when you leave to buy a soda and accidentally return to someone else's tee area.

Besides practice, the driving range is a nice place to impress those who never get to see you in action on the course. If they don't know the game at all, a 230-yard slice into the nearby batting cages looks impressive. This is also your chance to try and indoctrinate your spouse into the game without holding up the next dozen foursomes on the course. If you want to encourage or discourage them from taking up the game, this is your opportunity. Let them hit a few. If they're doing well and having fun, show them the interlocking grip—that'll discourage 'em. If they're doing poorly, give them the 7 iron so they'll pop a few 30 feet in the air—if you want to encourage them. Simply put, the driving range gives you the opportunity to turn someone on or off to golf—use this power wisely!

The Great Deception

Why Do You Always Hit Better at the Driving Range?
A Comparison

Driving Range	On the Course
1. You look out and see giant distance markers that aren't very hard to reach	1. You look out and see lots of hazards that ARE very hard to miss.
2. You don't have to see where it lands.	2. You may not want to see where it lands.
3. You can take 100 shots if you like.	3. You can take 100 shots and wanna shoot yourself.
4. You can experiment with different stances and grips.	4. You can pray that you've finally found a stance and a grip that you like.
5. You can try to correct your slice.	5. You can hope your slice doesn't kill anyone.
6. If you hit a bad shot, you can simply hit the next one.	6. If you hit a bad shot, it is your next one.
7. There's no scorecard.	7. You wish there was no scorecard.
8. You don't have to worry about landing on the green.	8. You don't have to worry about landing on the green.

Miniature Golf

Miniature golf is basically a dreaded experience for anyone who plays the game for real. Nevertheless, it has a wide appeal for youngsters, families, and for couples dating. On a well-balanced miniature golf course (one on which the holes don't slant dramatically to the left or right), a legitimate golfer should be able to do whatever is required by the course creator with relative ease. It's embarrassing for anyone who shoots in the 80s at Pebble Beach to lose at miniature golf to a precocious nine year old.

There are no world-renowned miniature golfers, and its competitions are never televised, which further negates the myth that it will soon be an Olympic event. So for the mere fun of it, here are the basic rules to follow if you choose to indulge your family or friends and venture out onto the mini-links. Don't forget, you're the golfer, so you're in charge.

MINIATURE GOLF RULES: FOR "THE REAL GOLFER"

1. Try not to mix up the color of your ball and your opponent's on every hole.
2. On uphill holes, the first three or four shots that roll back down to your feet don't count. Mulligan's are "in vogue."
3. Remind your fellow players that the maximum is five per hole, otherwise you'll be on the mini-links for the rest of your life.
4. Don't bring your own putter—everyone will want to use it.
5. When writing your name on the miniature barn, windmill, or farmhouse, use a black marking pen.
6. Leave your bag at home.
7. Make an effort not to get too wrapped up in watching the people on the driving range.
8. If, while you're waiting for the next hole, you use your "rented" club to get into a spirited hockey match, it's polite to let others play through.
9. When approaching the course from the parking lot, should you see two small children, their mother, and grandmother heading to the course ahead of you, run to the window, pay the fee, and get to the course ahead of them.
10. No, you can't stop the windmill to take a shot.
11. If you land in a position where you can't make your ball go around the metal contraption on the loop-the-loop hole in a brilliant display of centrifugal force, start the hole over.
12. Yes, it's okay to move the

ball two clubheads and a shoe away from the side if it's against the wooden partition for the hole or against an obstacle—or if you just feel like it.

13. Don't start teaching the overlapping grip.

14. If you win a free game, give it to someone else, but keep the pencil.

A Few of the Tournaments

THE MCDONALD'S OPEN—It's the only tournament where, after a caddie hands you your club, he'll ask "Do you want fries with that?"

•

THE JEAN DIXON CELEBRITY OPEN—They post the winners before starting.

•

THE WEIGHT WATCHERS CLASSIC—It's the only tournament where the refreshment stand is considered a hazard.

•

THE SAUDI ARABIA OPEN—95 percent sand trap.

•

THE JAMIE FARR INVITATIONAL—The only LPGA tournament where the host dresses in drag to participate.

•

THE BMW CLASSIC—The hell with the score, you'll love their carts.

•

THE SOCIETY FOR SUPERSTITIOUS GOLFERS CLASSIC—No 13th hole.

•

THE SARA LEE DESSERT CLASSIC—Dessert after each hole. Nobody doesn't like this one, and nobody ever finishes.

•

THE COLORADO SPRINGS ALL-NUDE INVITATIONAL—This is one tournament where you can tell a person's handicap just by looking at them.

•

THE OPTOMETRISTS' OPEN—Every year they play at the same club and spend hours deciding whether to play course number one or course number two.

•

THE JIMMY THE GREEK CLASSIC—Odds posted at every hole.

•

THE INTERNAL REVENUE AGENTS' CLASSIC—They don't play very well, but the scores are always accurate.

•

THE MERRILL LYNCH OPEN—You think bunkers are tough, try chipping around a few bulls.

•

THE COUCH POTATO INVITA-
TIONAL—It's televised so no
one ever shows up.

●

THE ROGER RABBIT CELEB-
RITY CLASSIC—The first ani-
mated tournament. If you
don't like a shot you can erase
it.

●

THE LAWNSMEN OF AMERICA
OPEN—They take forever re-
placing divots.

●

THE MAXWELL HOUSE OPEN—
Good till the last putt drops.

What's an SS in Golf?

Yes, even golf has gone statistic
crazy in recent years. Fortunately, no one has yet devised
a rotisserie golf tournament, but
it's probably coming soon. If you
follow the numbers game, like in
baseball, there are a lot more
categories being mentioned on
the pro tour these days. A mere
score is no longer the whole
story. Here are only a few of the
latest statistics that you may
find yourself keeping on your
own game.

SA (SCORING AVERAGE)—If
Michael Jordan can score
over 30 points per game in the
NBA, then it makes perfect
sense to see who's averaging
68 on the PGA tour, or how
you're doing.

RS and RS PCT—Here we have
how many rounds golfers have
shot in the 60s and their percentage from all the rounds
they've played this year, or
month, or week, or over the
weekend, or ever, depending
on what you're looking for and
who has the patience to look
it up.

SS (SAND SAVES)—Yes, it's a
real statistic.

CPS (CART PATH SAVES)—In
another year.

PPG (PUTTS PER GREEN)—The
difference between Greg Nor-
man, an 8 to 1 favorite to win
the 1990 U.S. Open, and an
amateur 100 to 1 long shot
was 1.75 to 1.79. Important
stat? We think not.

NCA (NEW CLUBS ADDED)—
You've replaced your 5 wood
with a 4 wood? The statisti-
cians want to know.

WC PCT (WRONG CLUB PER-
CENTAGE)—Since you can't
keep stats on yourself, you'll
need someone else to keep
track of how many times you
used the wrong club. Only ask
for the total when you're leaving the course for the day.

RP (ROUNDS UNDER PAR)—
Here's one most Sunday golfers will need a good stat man
to keep for them.

RN (ROUNDS UNDER 90)—
That's more like it!

EXPR (EXCUSES PER ROUND)
—Fewer than 21 excuses for
bad shots is considered a
good day.

PCT CT (PERCENTAGE OF
CLUBS THROWN)

TRH PCT (TREES HIT PER-
CENTAGE)—Not based on
number of shots but on number of trees—basically to see
if you missed any.

BL (BALLS LOST)

BL PCT—Percentage of balls
lost out of how many you
started the round with.

SCT (SCORECARD CHECKING
TOTAL)—Total number of
times you looked at the scorecard during the round and
wished you could play two or
three holes over.

TSTQ (NUMBER OF TIMES
YOU'VE SWORN TO QUIT)—
during a given round.

These are just a few of the stats
you might want to keep on yourself and on your most frequent
partners on the course.

7th HOLE—

"Real" Golfers

> You don't know what pressure is until you play for five bucks with only two in your pocket.
>
> —Lee Trevino

Are You a Trooper? Can You Brave Any Course and Any Elements?

WHAT TESTS A "REAL" GOLFER?

HOW ROUGH IS THE ROUGH?

1. Is the grass so thick that a cart that strayed from the path is now being towed out?
2. Is the Army using the underbrush to conceal a missile launcher?
3. Is the grass taller than your 9 iron?
4. Has the grass reached the point where the weeds have weeds?
5. Is there a film crew in the foliage making a Tarzan movie?

HOW WINDY IS WINDY?

1. Did your 90-yard 9-iron chip shot on the 5th just whiz by the gang walking off the green on the 17th?
2. Has your putt already started toward the hole without you?
3. Has your hat just outdistanced your shot by 100 yards?
4. Was that your handcart that just passed you as you started your backswing?
5. Is the glove from your back pocket now some 40 miles outside of downtown Duluth?

HOW RAINY IS RAINY?

1. Is the course pro rounding up golfers in pairs of two?
2. Did someone just say, "The hell with what club, what bait should we use?"
3. Did your caddie just hand you "soap on a rope"?
4. Are salmon swimming up the fairway to spawn?
5. Are you having trouble discerning the water hazards?

HOW STEEP IS STEEP?

1. Are Olympic skiers practicing on the same "hill"?
2. Are the golf carts equipped with low gear?
3. Did you just yell "Fore" at a mountain goat?
4. Does the only way to get to the green involve rope climbing?
5. Does the flagstick have a flashing red light for airplanes?

HOW COLD IS COLD?

1. Has your ball frozen to the tee?
2. Have other golfers tried to climb into your golf bag?
3. Did the grounds keepers just torch your cart to keep warm?

4. Did the shaft on your 3 iron just snap upon impact?
5. Are you wearing a fourth pair of socks over your golf shoes?

HOW HOT IS HOT?

1. Did sparks just fly from your last iron shot?
2. Are golfers taking their carts back to the clubhouse to have air-conditioning installed?
3. Do more people seem to be intentionally playing into the water hazards?
4. Are vendors getting blank checks for cold beer?
5. Are both men and women playing the literal version of the "Skins" game?

HOW FAST IS A "FAST" GREEN?

1. Did your last putt leave skid marks?
2. Does a good pitch with bite still end up in a nearby ravine?
3. Are putts being measured with a speed gun?
4. Are film crews using slow-motion replays to show the putting?
5. Is the green so dry that it should be called the brown?

HOW SLOW IS A "SLOW" GREEN?

1. Are other golfers taking a full backswing on their putts?
2. Are frogs jumping over the ball in motion?
3. Did your last attempted 10-foot putt stop at your front foot?
4. Are others in front of you not even bothering to mark their balls, knowing that you'll never reach them anyway?
5. Is there enough water on the green that if you add a bouillon cube you'll have soup?

HOW TOUGH IS A "TOUGH" COURSE?

1. Have Palmer, Nichlaus, and Trevino walked off relieved after shooting in the mid-80s?
2. Do hazard include vermin, locusts, and tribal warriors?
3. Are there really five uphill 570-yard par 5s complete with water hazards, bunkers, narrow fairways, and a treacherous underbrush?
4. Do many golfers switch to tennis after attempting the front 9?
5. Are the course regulars referred to as kamikaze golfers?

Roughing It

After your shot lands in the rough and you've cursed appropriately, you get to check out your lie. Basically you can expect one of three things: (1) Your ball is sitting up and you have a flier, or a good lie; (2) your ball is entrenched in the thick grass; (3) your ball has dug its way so deeply into the grass that a lawn doctor may be needed to surgically remove it.

In the first situation, a good lie, you can expect your ball to fly, and your shot may run more than your eggs did at breakfast. In the second situation, you'll want to hit the grass directly be-

hind the ball with a 4 iron or croquet mallet. With the thick grass, it feels like you're hitting the ball with a dinner roll. In the third situation, you may want a priest to administer last rites to your ball.

In the rough it's a good idea to take practice swings for three simple reasons: (1) You'll get a feel for the terrain; (2) you may "inadvertently" nudge the ball onto a better lie; (3) you could throw your back out and not have to take the next shot.

It's also advised that, when in the rough, take a slow backswing to give yourself a moment for prayer. You should also be sure to accelerate your swing at and through impact. Then accelerate yourself to find and pick up the club as it follows the ball toward the bunker.

A Few Forgotten Duffers

Here are just some of the infamous lot who should be remembered in golfing history. Along with those who've dazzled us in the Opens, these duffers should be remembered.

Wrong Way MacLemore

Wrong Way, an amateur at best, got his nickname in the late 1950s for his consistent ability to play the wrong hole during local tournament play in his hometown of Austin, Texas. No matter where the others went, Wrong Way somehow managed to follow the 4th hole with the 16th, the 7th with the 3rd, and so on. The oddity was that whenever Wrong Way played the course out of sequence, his game improved dramatically. He was, however, banned from local tournaments for causing constant confusion.

Banished from competition in his hometown, Wrong Way picked up and moved to Long Island, New York, where he once again entered local tournaments. His old habit returned, and before long he found himself veering off and playing the wrong holes. This time, however, before the regularity of his misguided adventures became widespread, Wrong Way consulted with club presidents at nine different clubs and urged them to routinely change the number and direction of their courses every so often. He tried to convince them that it would be an exciting new challenge if players found the course altered from week to week. This way, he figured, other golfers would be quite understanding if he chose the wrong direction—it would seem only natural. Wrong Way, however, struck out in his bid to alter the system. He did, however, manage to persuade one architect to build a course without numbers, whereby golfers could keep on playing by moving on to one of several next holes until they had played a total of 18.

The architect convinced one club owner in need of a gimmick for additional membership. Thus, Wrong Way had the perfect course, one on which he and other golfers could journey randomly from hole to hole until they'd played 18 (hopefully different) holes. For one season the course was a hit, but little by little golfers found a need for order and sequence. Fifteen golfers would be ready to play the 7th hole, while people rarely ventured to 5 or 6. Players were teeing off from tee areas for the wrong holes. It was getting out of hand and dangerous. Finally, the holes were put in order, and because Wrong Way had become quite chummy with the architect, he had a little say in that final order. Unfortunately, as time went on, Wrong Way once again veered in other directions until he was finally banished from yet another course. Wrong Way did, however, save up enough money to have three holes built beside his Long Island home. Neighbors claim that he never plays them in the same order twice in a row.

Sol and Gladys

Nobody recalls exactly what their last name was, but Sol and Gladys were legends on the monster course at the Concord, not to mention Kutsher's, the Pines, and other Catskill resorts. What made this couple (married 43 years) so unique was that they played as a team. Sol used the woods, the 2, 3, and 4 irons, whereas Gladys was proficient with the 5, 6, and 7 irons; he handled the 8 and 9, she used the wedges and always hit out of the sand; for putting, it depended on the greens—he hit on slow, she hit on fast.

Normally this would never have been allowed to happen, except that they were playing, as a team, in the low 80s and becoming a drawing card for their activities. Nonplayers would spend extra time and money around the clubhouse and at the snack bars just to watch them play a hole or two. Pretty soon, the resorts realized it was in their best interest to give them free weekends in exchange for advertising "The Golfing Couple."

They dressed in matching outfits, carried one bag, and often argued while approaching the ball. This added to their charm, and the crowds loved it. In fact, they became so well known that other couples thought it was the way to keep their marriage fresh—play golf together—as a team. Naturally this proved a disaster, as groups of eight now stood at the tee areas, and bickering couples could be heard from bunkers all over the course. "No. I hit the 5 iron." "No, no, I'm

better out of the rough than you are!" "Hey, the wedge is my shot!" These were the arguments ringing from the links.

Finally, couples were storming off the courses enraged at one another and, more often than not, one of the pair was divoting up the whole course! Resorts throughout the mountains stopped allowing this newfound husband and wife teaming up. The rules were clear: two bags two players, and so on.

Thus the fleeting fame of Sol and Gladys came to an end. They did, however, keep up their one-two punch on some of the courses. By slipping a ten spot to a few other golfers to keep quiet, Sol would then sneak Gladys onto the course on or about the 2nd hole, after it appeared that he'd gone out on the course himself. Then, on 17 she'd kiss him goodbye, and Sol was on his own again. Other than the first and last holes, they still did great as "The Golfing Couple."

Jerry Waxx—The Hit-and-Run Golfer

Jerry played for 20 years until his untimely death at the age of 59. He was a traveling salesman who visited a town briefly and stopped by a course once—and only once. As it were, he could never come back. Using the term "Hit and Run" Jerry did not mean with his shot, but rather in the manner used to describe an accident. Jerry had a passion for the game, so much so that he felt insulted by the idea of paying a greens fee or membership to play.

Thus, Jerry perfected a way of either being struck by a ball, a cart, a club, or if necessary, a car in the parking lot. He got to play for free and often dine for free on many of the most challenging and exclusive courses in the world.

Jerry would stop at nothing. If he couldn't get on a course he'd merely say he was inquiring about membership then manage an accident in the pro shop. It was rare that a club president or local pro didn't invite him back as their guest for a free round—and lunch or even dinner. He probably could have kept his scheme going well into his seventies if he didn't attempt one accident just a drop too close to the cliffs overlooking the Pacific Ocean. Jerry was heard yelling as he fell, "I'll sue the clubhouse out from under you."

That marked the tragic end of Jerry "Hit-and-Run" Waxx, but as you probably guessed, the West Coast club did foot the bill for his funeral.

8th HOLE—

Off the Course

You can apply a lot of things from golf to life. Go at your own pace, do your best, concentrate on the here and now, and keep your head down.

—Deborah Harmon,
    actress (*Used Cars,*
    Bachelor Party,
    TV's "Just the Ten of Us")

Night Clubbing

Since it's not easy finding a course that's well lit for night play, golfers need to fill their evenings with other activities. Evening favorites include the driving range, watching a taped playback of the afternoon's televised PGA event, reading about improving your game with tips from the pros, or sleeping.

Shopping might be your spouse's idea, but if you go, choose a mall, preferably one with a sporting goods store, or at least a bookstore with a few golf books. If you're really strapped, maybe you can seek out a toy store and fondle the computer golf games.

Both single and married golfers like to spend their evening seeking out a duffer of the opposite sex with one of many classic golf pick-up lines such as the following.

Ladies, try these:

"Is that a putter in your pocket or are you just glad to see me?"

"Since I've been watching you, I've been experiencing casual water."

"I'll bet your balls are Top Flite."

Gentlemen, these should work:

"I was just admiring your backswing."

"You look like the kind of lady who appreciates a good lie."

"Want to come back to my place and do some night putting?"

Should you find yourself getting intimate with a golfer, you can usually turn them on by holding them with an overlapping grip. Many golfers also find it stimulating to wear a visor during foreplay.

Whatever you do, golf at night is basically a thing of the future unless you play in Alaska or inside a Denny's. Someday they will probably perfect the Day-Glo golf ball along with illuminated fairways and floodlights on the green. A few flashing lights around the hazards and you'll be all set—provided, of course, your cart has headlights and the trees are painted a bright color. Until then, nightime is the wrong time to be with the game you love.

Sex and the Single Golfer

Here are some ways in which you can tell if your favorite golfer is worth playing around with, when they're not busy playing a round.

For the ladies, here are several things to watch for in that male golfer you've set your sights on.

1. Notice whether, on his interlocking grip, his fingers wrap

around the club twice. If so, you may be in luck.

2. Note whether he takes practice strokes before just sticking his tee in the ground.
3. Does he have a slow backswing, or does he just hurry through everything?
4. After taking his ball from the cup does he linger around the green or hurry off to play the next hole?
5. Is he modest about his game, or does he tell everyone in the clubhouse about his every stroke?

Men, here are a few things you might watch for in the female golfer you fancy.

1. Does she have nice "form"?
2. Does she grip the club well, as though she's familiar with it?
3. Does she keep her head down?

Is Golf Ruining Your Marriage?

For the Ladies

Here's a test for ladies who don't play "The Game" and wish their spouses didn't either. Are you a golf widow?

1. **On your last wedding anniversary you:**
   A. Had a romantic dinner in some out-of-the-way restaurant
   B. Had a somewhat romantic dinner at the country club overlooking the back nine
   C. Received golf lessons

2. **At 5 A.M. your husband:**
   A. Wakes you up to fool around
   B. Leaves the house to play a round
   C. Destroys the kitchen in his feeble attempt to find the breakfast of champions

3. **Your husband receives a bonus from the office. He uses the money:**
   A. To repave the driveway
   B. To buy you a new outfit
   C. To buy a new 3 wood
   D. To buy a 90-minute videocassette called "Great Moments in Golf 1890–1990"

4. **Your living room carpet:**
   A. Is a plush shag
   B. Has divots from chip-shot practice
   C. Is AstroTurf

5. **While asleep your husband:**
   A. Tosses and turns
   B. Talks
   C. Walks
   D. Replaces divots

6. **On your last vacation:**
   A. You met another lovely couple
   B. Your husband met three other men who played "The Game," and you didn't see him for a week
   C. You phoned home to see if he had at least quit when the sun went down

7. **Your husband gets excited when you:**
   A. Wear sexy lingerie and exotic perfume
   B. Strike a seductive pose on the bed
   C. Hold up a flag and smell like freshly-cut grass

8. **Your family photo album has a dozen pictures:**
   A. From your trip to Europe
   B. Of your daughter's graduation
   C. Of your husband's grip, backswing, and stance

9. **In searching for a new home, your husband wants one that:**
   A. Is convenient for shopping
   B. Is accessible to his office
   C. Is near at least three courses and a driving range
   D. Is surrounded by sand, entirely green, has a small pond in the middle and flags on the roof

Is Golf Ruining Your Marriage?—

For Married Couples Who *Both* Play

1. **During an argument, your spouse hits below the belt by mentioning:**
   A. Your relatives
   B. Your filthy habits
   C. Your triple bogey on the 18th

2. **If you have another child, you'd like to name it:**
   A. After a family member who golfs
   B. After the course where you sunk that 40-foot putt for an eagle
   C. Fuzzy

3. **You don't like to get together with your spouse's friends because they:**
   A. Don't know a 3 wood from a 3 iron
   B. Think squash is the best game around
   C. Can't understand why you want to call it a night at 9 P.M. on Saturday
   D. All of the above

4. **Your spouse's biggest complaint about you is:**
   A. You're dishonest
   B. You're insincere
   C. You're not trustworthy
   D. You don't keep your head down

5. **You feel your spouse should compliment you more often on:**
   A. Your business success
   B. Your appearance and physique
   C. Your short game

6. **You feel you're growing apart because:**
   A. You don't like the same television shows.
   B. One of you is a Democrat and the other a Republican
   C. One of you uses an overlapping grip, whereas the other uses an interlocking.

Golf on TV

Golf is a unique television sports experience because it's covered in a manner quite different from that of any other sport. If you want to follow a player through a tournament, forget it. Golf picks up the tournament leaders and moves you from hole to hole in an occasionally dizzying manner. Sure, it's much more fun to watch the shots than the players walking down the fairway, but there are times, thanks to the magic of television, that you'll see Fred Couples tee off, suddenly pick up Nick Faldo's ball in flight, and before you realize it, Tom Kite has holed out. If you're not following closely it looks like they teamed up to get an eagle.

Besides testing the "green" on your television, golf is a test of your hearing because the announcers whisper. Turning the volume up is a nice idea, but since the commercials don't whisper, you'd better be quick on the remote mute button. People ofter ask why golf announcers whisper. Are they actually that close to the players? Generally they're not, but they want you to feel the serene "golf" atmosphere while watching. This may be difficult if someone is vacuuming in the next room.

Nongolfers generally can't understand how anyone could watch golf on TV. It may be true that televised golf doesn't have the riveting, fast-paced excitement of a daytime soap, but it has its own brand of tension and drama. Viewers find themselves wondering who will win, who will hit one that will have the gallery running for cover, which episode of "The Three Stooges" will air if they get rained out, and will the network coverage last until the end of the day's play or will they break in with the film *Heidi* or the local evening news.

Good golf coverage will check in frequently on the Leader Board so that you can ask yourself at home: "Seven under? How do they do that?" Fortunately, good coverage will also fill you in on those who didn't make the cut. This is to give you that instant of gratification knowing that top pros didn't make the cut—just as you wouldn't have: "See, they have bad days too." Of course, you'd kill for one of their "bad" rounds.

One of the toughest things about watching televised golf is that you can't help but imagine that with just a little practice and a few adjustments on your game, you can play as well as they do. After all, they're using clubs that look like yours, standing in a manner similar to you, using the same kind of ball, and even wearing clothes that you yourself own!

While defending your right to watch golf, you will inevitably find yourself using the familiar— "I can really learn something from watching these guys." Although it sounds good, basically all you will really learn is that there are actually people (not many—that's why they're on TV) who don't regard "PAR" as some fictitious component in the over-all scheme of things.

The Big Switch

GOLF VERSUS TENNIS

Why are so many tennis players making the switch to golf?

LET'S COMPARE

1. While waiting to tee off or walking along the fairway, it's far easier to discuss a business transaction than trying to fast-talk your op-ponent into a new fiscal strategy while waiting for a lob to land on the court.
2. Tennis courts—clay, grass, or even cement—are essen-tially the same size with the same boring straight lines. Choosing a court is like buy-ing a home in a neighbor-hood featuring 200 identical row houses. Eighteen courts side by side are identical, but 18 holes on the course look different, each present-ing a new challenge or tor-ture—and isn't variety the spice of life?
3. Tennis tolerates the rant-

ings and ravings of its top players. Professional golf-ers don't throw nationally televised tantrums—they wait until they're alone.
4. Fuzzy is a more fun name than Bjorn was.
5. You can't build a condomi-nium on a tennis court.
6. Michael "Air" Jordan plays golf!
7. You have time to savor a good shot on the golf course, whereas in tennis there's no time to appreci-ate your fine work.
8. Tennis courts in Hawaii are no more or less "breathtak-ing" than those in Akron, Ohio.
9. You don't have to deal with sharp metal air-tight cans for golf balls, just cello-phane.
10. In golf you get to keep all sorts of neat stuff in your golf bag. How much can you cram into a tennis racket cover?

10 Reasons Why Baseball Players Like Golf

1. No umpires.
2. Less chance of needing ar-throscopic surgery.
3. Something to do during those long player strikes.
4. Something to talk about in

the broadcast booth during a pitching change.

5. Considerably less chance of being struck out or pinch hit for.
6. They don't show your worst shots nine more times on the DiamondVision scoreboard.
7. There's no stupid balk rule.
8. You don't have to listen to 16 choruses of "We Will Rock You" every day.
9. There's less peer pressure to spit.
10. Fans rarely chant "Darryl."

How to Really "Tee Off" a Golfer

Have you ever been in the midst of a quarrel, and your spouse, boss, lover, father, mother, or religious leader has left to play golf? Are you, for any reason, seeking revenge with afficionados of "The Game"? Here is a list of rotten things to do to golfers. This list may also come in handy if you're losing a match to a pompous opponent. Here's what to do:

1. Shorten their tees.
2. Inquire as to whether they inhale or exhale on their backswing.
3. Tighten the wheels on their cart.
4. Replace their new Top-Flites with balls freshly fished out of water hazards.
5. Make hand shadows in their line on the putting green.
6. While they're taking practice swings, point to their back foot, shake your head and walk away.
7. While they're concentrating on their shots, walk by within earshot carrying a pocket full of loose change.
8. Adjust their cap with Krazy Glue so that it is permanently one size too large.
9. Make footprints in the sand traps with a pair of Army boots.
10. Remove the flag while they're still approaching the green.

9th HOLE—

Potpourri

That's the tree I was aiming for.

—*Richard Mintzer*

Truisms

Here are some of the "realities" of this bizarre game.

Mrs. Arnold Palmer was once on the "Tonight Show," and when asked if she did anything special to help her husband's game, she replied innocently enough, "I kiss his balls." Johnny Carson, somewhat taken aback, retorted quickly, "And I'll bet that makes his putter rise."

In Kansas City, MO, there is a tournament called the Jim Smith Open. Oddly enough, it is open to anyone named Jim Smith. The least favored position in all of golf must be scoring this tourney. This is, however, the only tournament in which the trophy is engraved with the winner's name prior to the start of the event.

One of the most challenging tournaments is considered to be the Anheuser-Busch Classic in Virginia. With beer on tap from hole to hole the challenge isn't controlling your slice, it's controlling your bladder. This tourney adds a new meaning to the term *pitch and run*.

P. T. Barnum's old saying can now be adapted to golf— "There's a duffer born every minute." For this reason there is now an LBGA, the Laid Back Golfers Association. Members receive a certificate verifying them as "Way Over Par" players. However, players must pledge not to throw clubs, break clubs, or vent their wrath of the course on their spouses or friends.

After hitting a golf ball off the first tee through a large plate-glass window into the club-house, Former Detroit Lions linebacker Alex Karras walked over to a stunned grounds keeper of the Red Run Golf Club and asked, "Hey, is this room out of bounds?"

Can a family be too good at golf? In the 1956 Tasmanian Open the first three money winners were two brothers and their father. Their names were Peter, Alfred, and John Toogood. Who could make that up?

In the 1973 Indian Open in Delhi, a new hazard was introduced to the golf world—bees, in large numbers. To get rid of them the tournament officials created yet a second new hazard by lighting fires around the course. Not to be upstaged, organizers of the 1974 Indian Open seriously considered having players tee off while standing on a bed of nails or upon hot coals.

Orville Moody's daughter stopped caddying for him to

return to school. How often does one have the opportunity to give up a $100,000 a year position to start out in the world on her own?

According to the *Guinness Book of World Records* the lowest golf course in the world is at Kallia, by the shores of the Dead Sea. The course is 1,250 feet below sea level and is part of the Sodom and Gomorrah Golfing Society. Funny, most people didn't even know they played golf.

The *Guinness Book* also notes a Mr. Ian Colston of Victoria, an Australian who once played 401 holes of golf in one day, and we're not talking miniature golf, computer golf, or pitch and putt. Playing the 6,000-yard-plus course more than 22 times, he covered more than 100 miles. He also amassed the records for most mileage put on a golf cart in one day, most sand traps raked in one day, highest number of divots ever hit, most shots ever hit, most excuses used, most caddies yelled at in one day, and most times using these expressions: "Damn, I topped it," "I didn't allow for the break," and "My shorts are riding up on me." Rumor has it that he'd had a fight with his wife and was also quoted as saying, "I might not come home at all!"

There is now a putter, the Acculine PT-1000, which can stand on its own. Now if it could only putt on its own, it would outsell anything known to humanity.

One of the most popular sports among both professional jockeys and professional basketball players is golf. The latter, often using clubs that are longer than the former, frequently overhit the ball. The jockeys, although many play well, generally lack power. Could this be the first specialized golf team? One for the long game and one for the short?

Taking it too seriously? In the 1940s a pro named Ivan Gantz, while playing on the tour, missed a 3-foot putt. In a fit of anger Gantz flung his club upward. His club, however, was on target, whereas his shot hadn't been. The club struck Gantz on the head, knocking him unconscious. From this you learn two things: First, if you throw a club, get out of its path of flight, and second, an unconscious player on the green is considered an obstruction and may be moved.

During World War II a course in Scotland was used as an artillery range. Naturally, devout golfers played regardless. Thus a new rule was added to the course ground rules: "A player whose stroke is affected by the simultaneous explosion of a bomb or shell, or by machine-gun fire may play another."

If you've ever played a course that's given you a headache, how about one that can give you a hangover? Bordeaux, France, has a course where each of the 18 holes is named after a French vineyard. Anyone who gets a hole in one on the 5th hole—the par-3 "Pontet Canet"—wins a free bottle of wine. One can only guess that the tee area is marked by two white corkscrews sticking up from the ground.

One former PGA-er once received a check from a gentleman he did not know for $350, along with a short note explaining that the reason the pro couldn't find a ball he thought he'd hit well was because the man's wife had picked it up as a souvenir and walked off with it. Since the pro had finished third instead of second by one stroke, the husband felt guilty about his wife's action and sent him the monetary difference between second and third place. One can only speculate how much he had to repay the Show horse at the Kentucky Derby after this same wife walked off with a souvenir saddle.

It's worth giving credit where credit is due, and along those lines the "Candid Camera" crew put together some precious golf moments on the course—in the course of their many years on TV. Of note was the green with two holes, the green with no hole, the green with an extremely deep hole, and the green with a molasses surprise in the cup. There are those of us who'd still get a kick out of the quicksand sand trap, but we'll just have to hope some other show pulls that one off.

Golf Jokes

Two golfers were putting on the 17th green when one stopped for several moments to watch a funeral procession pass by. "Why the great interest in the procession?" asked one golfer.

"She was the best wife I ever had" replied the other.

Classic Golf Joke

MARTHA: "How was your game today, dear?"
JACK: "Awful. Fred dropped dead on the 2nd hole."
MARTHA: "Oh my God, that's terrible!"

JACK: "I'll say. All day it was take a shot, drag Fred, take a shot, drag Fred . . ."

In a recent pro-celebrity tournament one pro remarked, "I'm afraid to tell my partner about the 3rd hole. It's surrounded by water on three sides." A second pro responded, "Oh, I told my partner, and he guarantees we won't lose a ball."

"What cocky celebrity are you teamed up with?" asked the first pro.

"Jacques Cousteau."

ANDY: "Gerald Ford was the only President to hit 70."
RANDY: "Par?"
ANDY: "Spectators."

Every day at four o'clock, the grounds keepers at a country club in Iowa would drive their truck onto the course through an opening in a fence by the 2nd hole and proceed up a path near the green. Knowing this, one clever golfer bet that he could hit a 9-iron shot near the green on this 400-yard hole. Friends were eager to take this bet, knowing the impossibility of the feat. Thus at 3:57 the golfer fired a chip shot from the tee into the back of the truck, fully expecting that the truck's downhill route would deposit the ball next to the green. Sure enough, the truck turned through the gate and headed toward the 2nd green when suddenly the truck came to a halt before proceeding along its usual route. The angry golfer charged down the fairway shouting for the driver to continue. The driver stepped out and said, "We'd love to, but some nut just hit a ball through our gas tank."

After hitting three balls into the water the furious golfer flung the club into the water as well. "Damn caddy!" he screamed.

"What did he do?" asked his partner.

"He gave me the wrong club!" barked the golfer.

"What club was that?" inquired the partner.

The now more complacent golfer lifted his head and responded, "Yours."

Then there was the golfer who took a giant step while approaching his tee shot. After continuing this odd procedure for five holes, his caddy inquired as to what this giant step in his approach was all about. The player responded calmly, "My wife told me that if I plan to tee off tomorrow morning, it'll be over her dead body, so I'm practicing."

The company president was new at the game, so he took his assistant with him on the course. Every time the ball would veer from the fairway the assistant could be seen trying to find exactly where the shot landed. "Well," said the course pro to the executive after a decent 3-iron shot, "looks like your game is improving a little." "I sure hope so," said the chief exec. "My last three assistants drowned."

At 7 A.M., one of the worst golfers at the club was sauntering off the 18th green. "Wow," asked another club member, "what time did you start your round?" "About 4 P.M.," replied the duffer.

"So," said the doctor, "it appears that your blood pressure is normal and your cholesterol count is just fine." "Yeah, yeah, yeah," replied the aggravated patient, "but that still doesn't fix that hitch in my backswing."

The middle-aged man paid his money and entered the hotel room accompanied by a gorgeous prostitute. "Now" said the hooker, "I'm going to do things to you you've only dreamed of." "Really?" asked the customer excitedly. "You're gonna correct my slice?"

Before going under, the patient looked up and asked the anesthesiologist, "Has Dr. Walters been doing much operating lately?" "No," was the reply. "He's been on vacation, which is actually better for you." "You mean because he's relaxed?" questioned the patient. "No, but on vacation he plays a lot of golf, and it helps him remember to keep his head down when he's operating."

Then there was the guy who drove his car like his tee shots. On his back fender was a warning—Do not pass on right!

Why are more and more women saying they prefer golf to sex? Because golf always begins with four play.

During the throes of a miserable round, and after slicing two balls into a pond, the frustrated golfer was struck and killed by lightning. At the gates of heaven he asked, "Why'd you take me like that?" The gatekeeper looked at him and said, "We saw your game—we thought we were doing you a favor."

Golfers' License Plates

GLF2DAY   O 2 T UP

MR YIPS   GLFWIDO

Bumper Stickers

I BREAK FOR ANIMALS
BUT SINK BIRDIES

TRUE GOLFERS LOVE
TO PLAY AROUND

CAUTION: GOLFER AT THE
WHEEL/DRIVER IN TRUNK

GOLFERS RUN IN OUR FAMILY
I TEE OFF—THEY RUN

MY OTHER CAR IS A GOLF CART

DON'T BUG ME—I'M A GOLFER
I CAN TEE MYSELF OFF!

GOLFERS LOVE A 69

I MAY BE A DUFFER—BUT
I'M A DUFFER WITH A PORSCHE

PLAY "SAFE GOLF"
KEEP YOUR HEADS COVERED

Golf in the Future

By the year 2020 professional golfers should be winning about $10 million per tournament. Golf will be played mostly on AstroTurf, and foursomes will act as a team, utilizing the specialist idea from baseball and football whereby one player drives, one hits the iron shots, one is the chip-shot specialist, and then the "sort reliever" comes in to make the putt (often a miniature golf pro).

Players will be required to play all water hazards and will use the special "water wedge" club and appropriate "golf" scuba gear with matching visor. The state of Disney, formerly known as Florida, will hold the most tournaments, being the first climate-controlled state.

Your clubs will be hooked up to a portable computer, which will automatically gauge how far you are from the green and tell you where to stand. Caddies, a thing of the past, will be replaced by electronic bag movers, which will also clean your clubs for you.

Many golfers will use the slice-and-destroy method of play, whereby you are allowed to detonate an acutely sliced ball in mid-flight by the press of a button.

Those watching televised golf will be able to get into the game thanks to the "in-ball" lightweight camera. Because television will make a major impact on the game as it has on other sports, manmade hazards will represent the advertising dollars. Bunkers sporting soft-drink logos and colored sand traps displaying the colors of fast-food restaurants will be commonplace. New, TV-oriented hazards such as an overturned car or bikini-clad models sunning in the sand will enhance the growing TV audience.

As a result of new technology

in clubs and balls, 350-yard drives will be just average for a casual Sunday golfer. Therefore, what we know as par 4s will be par 3s, par 5s will be par 4s, and a par 5 will be roughly the state of Rhode Island.

Scary isn't it?